Homemade Bread

© Neuer Pawlak Verlag, a subsidiary of
VEMAG Verlags- und Medien Aktiengesellschaft, Cologne
www.apollo-intermedia.de

Picture credits: Neuer Pawlak Verlag, Cologne
Complete production: VEMAG Verlags- und Medien Aktiengesellschaft, Cologne
Printed in China

ISBN 3-86146-023-8

Homemade Bread

Fresh & Delicious

Contents

Bread and Rolls

The range of tasty breads and rolls on offer is sometimes quite overwhelming – by baking your own, however, you will top them all! Preparing the dough mixture becomes a pleasure as you look forward to the results, and the anticipation builds as the sweet scent of baking dough fills the room.

The following basic recipe is sufficient for a standard white loaf:

300 ml/10½ fl oz milk
40 g/1½ oz yeast
500 g/1 lb 2 oz plain flour
1 tsp sugar
1 tsp salt
40 g/1½ oz softened butter
Extras:
Flour, for preparation
Lard, to grease baking tray
Milk, for brushing loaf (if required)

The following recipe is sufficient for a large loaf or two small ones:

350 g/12 oz rye flour
350 g/12 oz whole grain wheatmeal
2 tsp salt
40 g/1½ oz yeast
1 tsp sugar
½ l/18 fl oz lukewarm water
150 g/5 oz (1 pkt) sour dough (ready-made)
Extras:
Flour, for preparation
Lard, to grease baking tray
Whole grain rye meal, to decorate

1. Prepare the ingredients to make a standard white loaf in an area where you can work at room temperature.

5. Pour the yeast milk mix into another bowl.

2. Heat the milk up gently, dissolve the yeast in it and leave to stand for 5 minutes.

6. Knead everything together using an electric mixer with kneading hooks until it becomes smooth and elastic.

3. Sift the flour into a mixing bowl.

7. Cover the bowl with cling film.

4. Add the sugar and salt to the flour and the butter in small clumps.

8. Leave the dough in a warm place to rise to double its original size. Then make any further preparations to the dough according to each recipe.

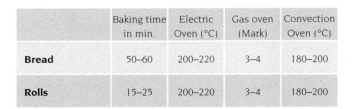

	Baking time in min.	Electric Oven (°C)	Gas oven (Mark)	Convection Oven (°C)
Bread	50–60	200–220	3–4	180–200
Rolls	15–25	200–220	3–4	180–200

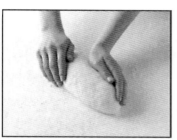

9. To make a standard white bread loaf pull and form the dough into a long loaf shape.

1. Measure out the ingredients for the sour dough bread, and lay them out ready for use.

5. Stir the rest of water into the leavened dough until well mixed.

9. Place the loaf or loaves on a greased baking tray and once again cover and leave to rise for a further 30 minutes.

10. Place on a greased baking tray and leave to rise for another 20 minutes.

2. Combine the flour and salt in a mixing bowl, and press a hollow into the middle using the back of a spoon.

6. Knead the dough thoroughly for 5–10 minutes.

10. Brush over the bread dough with water.

11. Then brush milk onto the leavened dough.

3. Crumble the yeast into the hollow and sprinkle over with the sugar.

7. Cover and leave again in a warm place to rise for approx. 30 minutes.

11. Make several diagonal cuts into the top of the bread using a sharp knife and sprinkle over with the rye meal.

12. Make about 4 diagonal cuts into the top of the dough with a sharp knife. Bake in a preheated oven.

4. Stir together with a little water, cover and leave to rise in a warm place for approx. 15 minutes.

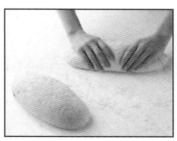

8. Knead the dough again thoroughly on a lightly floured work surface and form into a large loaf or two small ones.

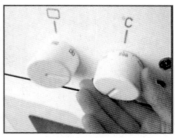

12. Bake in a preheated oven, together with an oven-proof bowl filled with water.

Types of Flour

Apart from a few exceptions, flour is the most important ingredient for baking recipes. Flour is produced in a milling process that involves grinding different kinds of grain. Good quality flour is dry and loose and will keep for long periods if stored in the right conditions. Ideally it should be kept in a sealed container and in a dry place. This will prevent it from losing its characteristic flavour and aroma. These days you don't have to sift flour due to stringent manufacturing processes that keep it free from by-products and vermin. You can however still sift it to create a lighter dough. Flour is a foodstuff that is naturally high in nutrients. The proportion of nutrient depends very much on how the grain is milled during manufacture. This is measured by the percentage of meal that results from a given amount of grain. Pay attention to the quality of the flour as described on the packaging. The proportion of the original whole grain that has been milled is decisive for the nutritional value.

Flour can be plain, wholemeal or whole grain. Ideally we should nourish ourselves with flour made from coarsely ground whole grain meal, due to the higher levels of protein, vitamins and minerals. The reason that fine flour is used for a lot of baked products is due to the fact that a lower percentage grain milling leaves them with more starch and as a result a better binding quality.

The modest cereal grain is quite a little miracle of nature. The minute seed is made up of numerous layers which hold a rich diversity in life giving nutritional substances that are distributed as follows:

Fruit husk
Contains fibre and minerals
Seed husk
Contains proteins and minerals
Aleuron layer
Contains protein and fat and rich in vitamins and ferments
Main seed (endosperm)
Contains carbohydrates
Germ
Contains vitamins, minerals, protein and germ oil

This seed structure is the same in all types of cereal, the nutritional value however varies slightly.

Wheat
Wheat is the most popular and widely used of all the cereals. Wheat flour is an indispensable ingredient for all sorts of baking. The fine flour types available are ideal for mixing with other ingredients to make light and even dough.

Average nutritional value for 100 g/3½ oz flour	Pertein g	Fat g	Energy kj	Potassium mg	Calcium mg	Phosphorus mg	Iron mg	B₁ µg	B₂ µg	Niacin mg
Wheat flour	10.6	1	1 523	100	15	90	1.5	70	30	2.57
Plain wheat flour	10.6	1.1	1 480	126	16	95	1.1	110	80	0.5
Wholemeal wheat flour	12.1	1.8	1 485	203	14	232	2.8	330	100	2.0
Wholemeal rye flour	7.4	1.1	1 453	240	31	180	2.3	190	110	0.8
Whole grain wheatmeal	12.1	2.1	1 465	290	41	372	3.3	360	170	5.0
Whole grain rye meal	10.8	1.5	1 432	439	23	362	3.3	300	140	2.9

Rye

After a long period of disuse, rye flour and milled rye products have become popular again. Particularly when used in wholemeal or whole grain form, rye will unveil its unique strong and nutty taste. This makes it ideal for hearty baked products, bread and bread rolls.

Buckwheat

Buckwheat is not a cereal but a type of knotgrass. Originating from the Russian steppes it made its way to Europe in the Middle Ages, as a kind of cereal for the poor folk. Since being revealed in more recent times as a highly nutritional foodstuff its value has obviously increased.

Spelt

Spelt can be seen as the predecessor to wheat and untreated it is also known as green corn, but is generally less associated with flour. It has, however, gained popularity recently due to the discovery that the grain is less affected by environmental pollution and pesticides. The explanation for this is the additional protective spelt husk that covers the grains and which must be removed before processing.

Hearty Bread

Westfalen Black Bread

For 1 loaf:
Dough:
750 g/1 lb 11 oz whole grain
rye meal
250 g/9 oz wheat flour
150 g/5 oz (1 pkt ready-made)
sour dough
$3/4$ l/pint 7 fl oz lukewarm water
1 tsp salt
20 g/$3/4$ oz yeast
Extras:
Flour, for preparation
Lard, to grease baking tray

1. Mix the rye meal with the wheat
flour. Add half of the meal mix to a
bowl and press down a hollow in
the middle of it.
2. Combine $1/2$ l/18 fl oz water with
the sour dough mixture and then
pour into the hollow. Mix together
with the rest of the meal and flour,
cover and leave overnight at room
temperature.
3. Add the rest of the water, the salt
and crumbled yeast to the dough
stirring and then kneading. Cover
again and leave to rise for about
3 hours.
4. Work the dough into a loaf shape
on a flour-covered work surface and
then place on a greased baking tray.
Leave to rise a little more for about
$1 1/2$ hours. Place on the middle shelf
of the preheated oven and bake.

Baking time:
approx. 1 hour 15 minutes
Electric oven: 200° C
Gas oven: mark 3
Convection oven: 180° C

Per 100 g approx. 5 g P, 1 g L, 37 g G =
190 kcal (798 kj)

Millet Bread with Sesame

For 1 loaf:
Dough:
130 g/4$\frac{1}{2}$ oz sesame seeds
350 g/12 oz wheat flour
400 g/14 oz millet flakes
42 g/1$\frac{1}{2}$ oz (1 cube) yeast
$\frac{1}{2}$ tsp sugar
$\frac{1}{2}$ l/18 fl oz buttermilk
3 tbsp water
2 tsp salt
75 ml/2$\frac{1}{2}$ fl oz hazelnut
or walnut oil
Extras:
Flour, for preparation
1 tbsp milk, for brushing

1. Dry roast 100 g/3$\frac{1}{2}$ oz of the sesame seeds in a frying pan stirring continuously until they are golden brown. Leave to cool.
2. Add the flour and millet flakes to a large mixing bowl and press down a hollow in the middle. Crumble the yeast into the hollow. Sprinkle over the sugar. Mix the buttermilk with the water and heat up gently then pour over the yeast to dissolve it. Sprinkle the roast sesame seeds, salt and oil over the outer edges of the flour. Working from the middle, knead all the ingredients into a smooth dough. Throw the dough on a flour-covered work surface, and then roll into a ball. Sprinkle with some flour and then cover and leave to rise at room temperature for 30–40 minutes.
3. Knead the dough thoroughly on the work surface and then roll to a 30 cm/12 in length. Sprinkle some flour into a long rattan bread basket. Press the dough roll into

the basket and leave to rise for another 30–40 minutes.
4. Remove the dough from the basket and throw onto a baking tray covered with greaseproof paper. Brush with the milk and sprinkle with the remaining sesame seeds. Place the loaf on the second shelf from the bottom of a preheated oven and bake with a cup of hot water on the lowest shelf.
5. Remove the ready loaf with the paper and leave to cool. Leave at least 8–10 hours before slicing.

Baking time: approx. 50 minutes
Electric oven: 200° C
Gas oven: mark 3
Convection oven: 180° C

Per 100 g approx. 11 g P, 13 g L, 39 g G = 322 kcal (1 348 kj)

Rice and Wheat Flour Bread

For 2 loaves:
Dough:
500 g/1 lb 2 oz rice
$\frac{1}{2}$ l/18 fl oz milk
2 kg/4 lb 7 oz wheat flour
50 g/1$\frac{3}{4}$ oz fresh yeast
1 tbsp salt
Extras:
1 egg yolk
Lard, to grease tray

1. Boil the rice in the milk until cooked through but still firm. Drain completely through a sieve. Add the flour to a large mixing bowl and fold in the rice while still warm, then press a hollow down into the middle.

2. Dissolve the yeast in 100 ml/ 3$\frac{1}{2}$ fl oz of lukewarm water and pour into the hollow. Cover and leave the dough mix to stand in a warm place for approx. 20 minutes.

3. Sprinkle over with the salt and begin to knead the dough adding drops of lukewarm water to keep it smooth. Cover the dough again and leave to rise for approx. 20 minutes.

4. Knead the dough again thoroughly and make into two separate loaf shapes. Whisk the egg yolk and brush over each loaf. Place on a greased baking tray and then straight into a preheated oven on the second shelf from the bottom. When ready baked place on a cake rack to cool.

Baking time: approx. 1 hour
Electric oven: 200° C
Gas oven: mark 3
Convection oven: 180° C

Per 100 g approx. 8 g P, 2 g L, 55 g G = 292 kcal (1 226 kj)

Hearty Dill Bread

For 1 loaf:
Dough:
100 g/3¹/₂ oz wholemeal rye flour
150 g/5 oz wholemeal wheat flour
42 g/1¹/₂ oz (1 cube) yeast
¹/₂ tsp sugar
80 ml/2³/₄ fl oz lukewarm milk
1 bunch of dill
1 small chopped onion
1 tsp salt • 2 tbsp soya oil
Extras:
Flour, for preparation
Lard, to grease baking tray
1 egg yolk
2 tbsp milk

1. Add the flour to a mixing bowl and press down a hollow into the middle. Crumble the yeast into the hollow, sprinkle over with the sugar and cover everything with the milk and leave to rise for 15 minutes. Wash and shake dry the dill, chop up finely and add to the flour together with the onion, salt and oil. Knead everything together until the dough doesn't stick to the sides of the bowl. Cover and leave to rise in a warm place for approx. 30 minutes.
2. Coat hands with flour and knead the dough once more on a flour covered work surface. Form the dough into a bread loaf. Place the

loaf on a greased baking tray and leave to rise for 15 minutes.
3. Make a lengthways slice about 1 cm/¹/₃ in into the loaf using a sharp knife. Whisk the egg yolk into the milk and brush onto the bread dough. Bake the bread in a preheated oven on the second shelf from the bottom.

Baking time: approx. 30 minutes
Electric oven: 225° C
Gas oven: mark 4
Convection oven: 200° C

Per 100 g approx. 7 g P, 10 g L; 34 g G = 275 kcal (1 155 kj)

Dark Rye Bread

For 1 loaf:
Dough:
$^1/_2$ l/18 fl oz water
125 g/4$^1/_2$ oz rye grains
(for cooking)
200 g/7 oz whole grain rye meal
200 g/7 oz whole grain wheatmeal
600 g/1 lb 5 oz wholemeal rye flour
25 g/1 oz salt
A sprinkle of salt
2 tsp molasses
60 g/2 oz yeast
250 g/9 oz soured milk
Extras:
Rye flour, for preparation
Lard, to grease tin
Whole grain wheatmeal, to dust
Water, to brush

1. Boil 125 ml/4$^1/_2$ fl oz water. Pour over the rye grain and leave to soak overnight.
2. Combine the whole grain rye and wheatmeal and the rye flour in a mixing bowl and press down a hollow into the middle. Sprinkle the salt, sugar and molasses around the edge. Crumble the yeast into the hollow. Heat the rest of the water (do not boil!), whisk in the soured milk and pour over the yeast. Wait for the yeast to dissolve and then working from the middle fold everything together and knead into a smooth dough. Add the soaked rye grains and knead in.
3. Sprinkle the dough with some rye flour, cover and then leave to rise in a warm place for approx. 45 minutes, until the dough has doubled in size.
4. Knead the dough onto a flour-covered work surface and roll into a ball. Cover once again and allow to settle for 8–10 minutes at room temperature. Grease a 35 cm/14 in

long loaf tin and sprinkle with whole grain wheatmeal. Roll the dough lengthways and press into the baking tin. Cover and leave to rise again for 10–15 minutes.
5. Brush the top of the loaf with water, sprinkle over with whole grain wheatmeal, and then cut notches along its length with a sharp knife.
6. Place a cup of hot water in the oven. Bake the bread in a preheated oven on the lowest shelf. Once ready remove the loaf from the baking tin carefully and leave to stand for at least 12 hours.

Baking time:
approx. 1 hour 15 minutes
Electric oven: 175° C
Gas oven: mark 2
Convection oven: 150° C

Per 100 g approx. 7 g P, 2 g L, 38 g G = 208 kcal (872 kj)

Rich Country Loaf

For 2 loaves:
Dough:
600 g/1 lb 5 oz whole grain rye meal
150 g/5 oz wholemeal rye flour
2 tsp salt
40 g/1 1/2 oz yeast
1 tsp sugar
1/2 l/18 fl oz lukewarm water
150 g/5 oz sour dough
(1 pkt ready-made)
100 g/3 1/2 oz pumpkin seeds
100 g/3 1/2 oz sunflower seeds
Extras:
Flour, for preparation
Lard, to grease baking tray
Whole grain rye meal, to sprinkle

1. Combine the whole grain rye meal, wholemeal rye flour, salt, yeast, sugar, water and sour dough and make into bread dough as described in the basic recipes at the beginning of this book.
2. Coarsely chop up the pumpkin and sunflower seeds and knead into the prepared dough.
3. Separate the dough into two portions and form each one, on a flour-covered work surface, into a loaf. Place the loaves on a greased baking tray and leave to rise for 30 minutes.
4. Brush the tops of each loaf with water, sprinkle with whole grain meal and make several 1 cm/1/3 in deep cuts using a sharp knife. Place on the middle shelf of a preheated oven and bake for the given time.

Baking time: approx. 1 hour
Electric oven: 200° C
Gas oven: mark 3
Convection oven: 180° C

Per 100 g approx. 9 g P, 3 g L, 34 g G = 224 kcal (943 kJ)

Roman Bread

For 1 loaf:
Dough:
40 g/1$^{1}/_{2}$ oz yeast
300 ml/10$^{1}/_{2}$ fl oz lukewarm water
$^{1}/_{2}$ tsp sugar
500 g/1 lb 2 oz plain wheat flour
1 tsp salt
1 bunch of basil
100 g/3$^{1}/_{2}$ oz raw ham
2 cloves of garlic
2 tbsp sour cream
Salt • Pepper
Extras:
Flour, for preparation
Lard, to grease the tin
1 egg yolk
2 tbsp milk

1. Crumble the yeast into the luke-warm water. Add the sugar, stirring well and leave to stand for 5 minutes.
2. Sift the flour into a bowl. Add the salt and yeast mix. Knead every-thing together into a smooth dough. Cover the dough and leave to rise to double its original size.
3. While waiting wash the basil, shake dry and chop up finely. Chop the ham into thin strips and chop the garlic up finely. Stir in the sour cream and season with the salt and pepper.
4. Place the yeast dough onto a flour-covered work surface and roll into a 15 x 25 cm/6 x 10 in rectangle.
5. Spread the herb and ham mixture onto the rolled-out dough and then roll it along the longest side.

6. Place the dough roll with the remaining edge facing down into a 25 cm/10 in long greased baking tin. Whisk the egg yolk and milk together and brush the bread with it. Bake on the middle shelf of a preheated oven for the given time.

Baking time: 40–45 minutes
Electric oven: 200˚ C
Gas oven: mark 3
Convection oven: 180˚ C

Per 100 g approx. 10 g P, 7 g L, 44 g G = 303 kcal (1 274 kj)

Malakoff (Russian Bread)

For 1 loaf:
Dough:
375 g/13 oz whole grain rye meal
375 g/13 oz wholemeal wheat flour
1 tbsp salt • 1 tsp sugar
1 tbsp caraway seeds
40 g/1 1/2 oz yeast
1/2 l/18 fl oz lukewarm water
150 g/5 oz sour dough
Extras:
Flour, for preparation
Lard, to grease the tray

1. Combine both the flour and meal with the sugar, salt and caraway seeds in a mixing bowl.
2. Crumble the yeast into the water, stir and leave to dissolve for approx. 5 minutes. Then pour it over the flour. Add the sour dough and then knead everything into a smooth dough. Cover and leave to stand for approx. 30 minutes.
3. Knead the dough again and leave to rise for a further 20 minutes.
4. Knead the dough on a flour-covered work surface into a round loaf form and then lay on a greased baking tray. Bake on the middle shelf of a preheated oven for the given time, brushing occasionally with water.

Baking time: approx. 1 hour
Electric oven: 220° C
Gas oven: mark 4
Convection oven: 200° C

Per 100 g approx. 12 g P, 3 g L, 58 g G = 332 kcal (1 398 kj)

Coriander Bread

For 1 loaf:
Dough:
400 g/14 oz plain wheat flour
600 g/1 lb 5 oz wholemeal
wheat flour
150 g/5 oz medium milled
buckwheat grain
2 tbsp ground coriander
1 tbsp salt
2 tsp sugar • 60 g/2 oz yeast
½ l/18 fl oz lukewarm water
100 g/3½ oz chopped walnut kernels
50 ml/1¾ fl oz walnut oil
Flour, to sprinkle

1. Combine all of the flour with the grain in a mixing bowl and press down a hollow into the middle. Sprinkle the salt and coriander around the edges. Dissolve the sugar and crumbled yeast in the lukewarm water and pour into the hollow. Add the walnuts and oil and then, working from the middle, knead the mixture into a smooth dough.
2. Cover and leave to rise at room temperature for 30–40 minutes or until the dough has doubled its original size. Knead again and allow to rise for a further 15 minutes. Knead the dough vigorously and

form into a loaf. Lay on a greased baking tray and dust with flour. Cut crosses into the top of the loaf.
3. Bake the bread in a preheated oven on the middle shelf. Leave to cool on a cake rack.

Baking time: 40–50 minutes
Electric oven: 200° C
Gas oven: mark 3
Convection oven: 180° C

Per 100 g approx. 10 g P, 8 g L, 62 g G = 348 kcal (1 453 kj)

Whole Grain Wheatmeal Bread

For 1 loaf:
500 g/1 lb 2 oz whole grain wheatmeal
250 g/9 oz plain wheat flour
1 ½ packets baking powder
A pinch of salt
½ l/18 fl oz buttermilk
50 g/1 ¾ oz butter or margarine
Flour, for preparation

1. Combine the whole grain wheatmeal, flour, baking powder and salt in a mixing bowl. Heat the buttermilk gently in a saucepan, and then pour into the middle of the flour mixture gradually and knead. Add the butter or margarine and knead until the dough is smooth.
2. Form into a flat round loaf and lay on a baking tray covered with greaseproof paper, then dust with flour. Make a large 1 cm/⅓ in deep cross into the top using a sharp knife.
3. Place on the middle shelf of a preheated oven and bake for the given time. Turn out onto a cake rack and leave to cool.

Baking time: approx. 35 minutes
Electric oven: 200° C
Gas oven: mark 3
Convection oven: 180° C

Per 100 g approx. 8 g P, 5 g L, 42 g G = 251 kcal (1 048 kj)

Tip
The amount of liquids given in the recipes tries to be as accurate as possible. Flour however varies in how much liquid it absorbs. If the dough crumbles while kneading then it needs more liquid and if it is too soft then add more flour. Good dough should be smooth but shapeable.

French Mustard Bread

For 1 loaf:
Dough:
100 g/3 $\frac{1}{2}$ oz butter or margarine
3 eggs
1 tbsp Dijon mustard
Freshly ground pepper
Salt
100 g/3 $\frac{1}{2}$ oz plain flour
40 g/1 $\frac{1}{2}$ oz yeast
100 g/3 $\frac{1}{2}$ oz cooked ham
100 g/3 $\frac{1}{2}$ oz mature Gouda
1 bunch of smooth parsley
1 bunch of estragon
Extras:
Lard, to grease the mould

1. Melt the butter or margarine in a pan. Whisk the eggs in a bowl while adding the Dijon mustard, pepper and salt. Stir in the melted fat while still warm. Gradually add the flour, stirring continuously with an electric mixer until a smooth dough is achieved. Cover the dough and leave to rise in a warm place for approx. 20 minutes.

2. Chop the cooked ham and cheese into small cubes. Wash and dab dry the parsley and estragon and chop up finely. Stir everything into the yeast dough and fill into a greased soufflé mould or similar ovenproof dish. Cover and leave to rise for another 15 minutes.

3. Bake the French mustard bread on the middle shelf of a preheated oven. Once baked leave to cool in the dish, and then tap out onto a plate and serve warm or lukewarm.

Baking time: approx. 40 minutes
Electric oven: 200° C
Gas oven: mark 3
Convection oven: 180° C

Per 100 g approx. 11 g P, 24 g L, 10 g G = 326 kcal (1 369 kj)

Quattro Bread

For 1 loaf:
Dough:
800 g/1 lb 12 oz plain wheat flour
250 g/9 oz whole grain wheatmeal
70 g/2 1/2 oz yeast • 1 tsp sugar
650 ml/1 pint 3 fl oz lukewarm water
1 tsp salt
2 tsp freshly ground pepper
1/4 l/9 fl oz walnut oil
Extras:
Flour, for dough preparation
Some water, for brushing
1. additional ingredient mix:
80 g/2 3/4 oz black olives (dried)
150 g/5 oz salami
2 tsp oregano
2. additional ingredient mix:
200 g/7 oz mature Gouda
2 tsp caraway seeds
1 tsp freshly ground pepper
3. additional ingredient mix:
100 g/3 1/2 oz hazelnut kernels
50 g/1 3/4 oz walnut kernels
4. additional ingredient mix:
100 g/3 1/2 oz pumpkin seeds
(shelled)
2 tsp ground coriander

1. Combine the flour and meal in a large mixing bowl and press down to make a hollow. Crumble in the yeast and sprinkle over the sugar. Pour the water over the yeast to dissolve it. Sprinkle the salt and pepper around the edges of the flour. Working from the middle, mix all the ingredients and knead into a smooth dough, while gradually adding the oil.

2. Roll the dough into a ball on a flour-covered work surface. Place the dough back into the bowl, dust over lightly with some flour, cover and leave to rise at room temperature for approx. 20–30 minutes or until the dough has doubled in size.

3. For the first additional ingredient mix, pit the olives and cut into quarters. Chop the salami into cubes. Mix together in a bowl with the oregano and place to one side.

4. For the second additional ingredient mix, chop the Gouda into small cubes, combine with caraway seeds and pepper and place to one side.

5. For the third additional ingredient mix, combine the hazelnuts and walnuts and place to one side.

6. For the fourth additional ingredient mix, combine the pumpkin seeds with the coriander and place to one side.

7. Roll the dough on a flour-covered work surface lengthways and cut into 4 equally sized portions. Knead the pre-prepared additional ingredients mixes into each portion of dough. Shape each portion into a pear shape, pinch the ends down flat and brush with water.

8. Lay each portion onto a baking tray covered with greaseproof paper, with each pointed end overlapping the other and join by pressing together.

9. Cover the bread with a tea towel and leave to rise for another 10 minutes. Then brush over with water and make three slices along the top of each quarter with a sharp knife. Bake on the second shelf from the bottom in a preheated oven. Remove and leave to cool on a cake rack before eating.

Baking time: 40–50 minutes
Electric oven: 200˚ C
Gas oven: mark 3
Convection oven: 180˚ C

Per 100 g approx. 9 g P, 22 g L, 31 g G = 372 kcal (1 553 kj)

Flat Bread

For 2 loaves:
Dough:
4 small chilli peppers
(15–20 g/ ¹/₂–³/₄ oz)
500 g/1 lb 2 oz wheat flour
25 g/1 oz yeast
A pinch of sugar
¹/₄ l/9 fl oz lukewarm water
3 tbsp olive oil
1 tsp salt

Extras:
Flour, for preparation
2 tbsp milk, for brushing
2 tbsp olive oil
2 tsp sesame seeds
2 tsp black caraway seeds

1. Slice off the chilli pepper stalks, cut them open lengthways and remove the seeds, wash and chop into small cubes.

2. Add the flour to a large mixing bowl and press down in the middle to make a hollow. Crumble the yeast into the hollow and pour the luke-warm water over it while adding the sugar and then leave briefly to dissolve. Add the olive oil, chilli peppers and salt to the edges of the flour. Working from the middle outwards knead everything into a smooth dough (you can use a mixer with a dough hook attached). Cover and leave to rise in a warm place for approx. 30–40 minutes until it has doubled its original size.

3. Knead the dough again on a flour-covered work surface and then separate into two halves. Roll each half into a ball, cover and allow to rise for a further 6–8 minutes.

4. Roll each ball out into a flat and round (20 cm/8 in diameter) or oval (15 x 30 cm/6 x 12 in) shape. Place on a baking tray covered with greaseproof paper. Cover again and leave for the last time to rise for at least 10–12 minutes.

5. Finally brush the flat bread with milk and dribble over with some olive oil. Sprinkle with sesame seeds and black caraway seeds and then place in a preheated oven on the second shelf from the bottom and bake for the given time. When ready remove from the oven and place on a cake rack to cool a little and then serve warm.

Baking time: approx. 20 minutes
Electric oven: 225° C
Gas oven: mark 4
Convection oven: 200° C

Per 100 g approx. 8 g P, 8 g L, 45 g G = 294 kcal (1 229 kj)

Spicy Flat Bread

For 1 flat bread:
Dough:
500 g/1 lb 2 oz plain flour
42 g/1 $\frac{1}{2}$ oz yeast
2 tbsp sugar • $\frac{1}{4}$ l milk
3 tbsp butter • 1 tbsp salt
Crust:
$\frac{1}{4}$ tsp ground ginger
3 tbsp roasted sesame seeds
2 tsp aniseed
2 tsp roasted caraway seeds
2 tsp poppy seeds
3 tbsp grated parmesan cheese
2 tbsp chopped pistachios
1 tbsp sunflower seeds • Salt
Pepper • 1 red bell pepper

1. Add the flour to a mixing bowl, press down a hollow into the middle and crumble the yeast into it.

2. Sprinkle over with a little of the sugar, then pour in the milk and allow the yeast to dissolve. Now add the rest of the sugar, chunks of the butter and the salt to the outer edges of the flour. Starting from the middle and working outwards knead everything into a smooth dough. Cover and leave to rise for approx. 1 hour.

3. Combine the ginger, aniseed, sesame, caraway and poppy seeds, cheese, pistachios and sunflowers seeds and stir together. Season well with the salt and pepper. Trim and wash the bell pepper then chop into small cubes.

4. Form the dough into a flat, round loaf and then sprinkle over the seed and spice mixture and the pepper cubes.

5. Bake the flat bread in a preheated oven on the middle shelf.

Baking time: approx. 40 minutes
Electric oven: 180° C
Gas oven: mark 2
Convection oven: 160° C

Per 100 g approx. 8 g P, 10 g L, 31 g G = 264 kcal (1 111 kj)

Three Grain Bread

For 1 loaf:
250 g/9 oz wheat grains
250 g/9 oz rye grains
500 g/1 lb 2 oz whole grain rye meal
250 g/9 oz coarse rolled oats
42 g/1 ½ oz (1 cube) yeast
1 tsp sugar
400 ml/14 fl oz lukewarm water
150 g/5 oz ready-made sour dough
3 tsp salt • 2 tsp aniseed
Whole grain rye meal, to sprinkle
Water, to brush
30 g/1 oz coarse rolled oats

1. Cover the wheat and rye grains with boiling water and leave to soak for 8 hours. Leaving them in the soaking water, boil for 2–3 minutes. Drain through a sieve and rinse with cold water.

2. Combine the soaked grains with the rye meal and oat flakes in a large mixing bowl, and then press a hollow down in the middle. Crumble the yeast into the hollow, sprinkle over with the sugar and then add 3 tablespoons lukewarm water to dissolve the yeast. Cover and leave to rise in a warm place for approx, 15 minutes.

3. Add the sour dough, remaining water, salt and aniseed. Knead everything into a smooth dough. Sprinkle a thin layer of rye meal on top, cover and leave to rise for 20–25 minutes.

4. Sprinkle some more meal onto a work surface, throw the dough onto it and then knead well. Form into an oval-shaped loaf approx. 35 cm/14 in long. Cover a baking tray with greaseproof paper and sprinkle some meal over it. Place the loaf onto the tray, brush with water and sprinkle the oat flakes on top.

5. Cover and leave to rise for a further 20–25 minutes. Place a cup of hot water on the bottom shelf of the oven. Bake the bread in a preheated oven on the second shelf from the bottom. Slide off the tray with the paper and leave to stand for 12 hours.

Baking time:
approx. 1 hour 10 minutes
Electric oven: 200° C
Gas oven: mark 3
Convection oven: 180° C

Per 100 g approx. 8 g P, 2 g L, 39 g G = 212 kcal (887 kj)

Greek Farmer's Bread

For 1 loaf:
Dough:
40 g/1 1/2 oz yeast
400 ml/14 fl oz lukewarm water
500 g/1 lb 2 oz plain wheat flour
100 g/3 1/2 oz Graham flour
5 tbsp olive oil • 2 tsp salt
15 black olives, pitted
Extras:
Flour, for preparation
Lard, to grease baking tray

1. Crumble the yeast in about 100 ml/3 1/2 fl oz lukewarm water and leave to soak for 10 minutes.
2. Combine the flour and Graham flour in a mixing bowl. Press down a hollow in the middle of the flour, and pour the yeast mix into it. Add the rest of the water, olive oil and salt and knead everything together into a smooth dough. Cover and leave the dough to rise to double its original size.
3. Knead the dough again, this time on a flour-covered work surface, and fold in the olives gradually. Form into a loaf shape and place onto a greased baking tray. Leave the

dough to rise for a further 30 minutes.
4. Bake in a preheated oven on the middle shelf. Brush water over the top of the loaf occasionally to stop it drying out.

Baking time: approx. 40 minutes
Electric oven: 200° C
Gas oven: mark 3
Convection oven: 180° C

Per 100 g approx. 6 g P, 5 g L, 33 g G = 227 kcal (955 kj)

31

Nutty Bread

For 2 loaves:
600 g/1 lb 5 oz whole grain rye meal
(coarse)
150 g/5 oz wholemeal rye flour
42 g/1$\frac{1}{2}$ oz yeast • 1 tsp sugar
450 ml/17 fl oz lukewarm water
150 g/5 oz ready-made sour dough
2 tsp salt
180 g/6$\frac{1}{2}$ oz walnut kernels
180 g/6$\frac{1}{2}$ oz hazelnuts
Whole grain meal, for preparation

1. Combine the rye meal and flour in a large mixing bowl and then press a hollow down in the middle. Crumble the yeast into the hollow. Pour the lukewarm water over the yeast and sprinkle with the sugar, then knead into a thin pre-dough, adding just a little flour. Cover with cling film and leave to rise at room temperature for approx. 15 minutes. Add 350–400 ml/12–14 fl oz luke-warm water, the sour dough and salt to the risen dough. Knead every-thing into a smooth dough using the kneading hooks on a mixer. Sprinkle a thin layer of whole grain meal on top, cover and once again leave to rise for approx. 1 hour.

2. Remove the dough from the bowl and then knead in the walnuts leav-ing some for decorating with after-wards. Break the dough into 2 halves and form into two loaves on a work surface sprinkled with whole grain meal. Brush some water over the bread loaves and then press the remaining walnut kernels into them. Sprinkle over some whole grain rye meal.

3. Place the loaves onto a baking tray covered with greaseproof paper and leave to rise for 30 minutes.

4. Place a cup of hot water on the bottom shelf of the preheated oven and bake the bread loaves on the second shelf from the bottom. Slide off the tray with the paper, place on a cake rack and leave to cool. Leave for at least 8–10 hours before slicing.

Baking time: approx. 55 minutes
Electric oven: 200° C
Gas oven: mark 3
Convection oven: 180° C

Per 100 g approx. 9 g P, 15 g L, 33 g G =
309 kcal (1 295 kj)

Coriander Herb Bread

For 1 loaf:
Dough:
1 small sprig of rosemary
1 small bunch of marjoram
1 small sprig of lovage
2 bunches of basil
2 bunches of chives
3 cloves of garlic
1 tbsp oil
500 g/1 lb 2 oz whole grain wheatmeal (coarse)
250 g/9 oz wholemeal wheat flour
42 g/1 ½ oz yeast • A pinch of sugar
3 tsp herb salt
1 tsp freshly ground pepper
½ l/18 fl oz Kefir (fermented milk)

Extras:
Flour, for preparing the dough
1 tbsp milk
2 tsp coriander seeds

1. Pick the rosemary and marjoram off their branches. Wash and if necessary shake dry the lovage and basil. Chop all the herbs up finely. Chop the chives into small rings and add to the rest of the herbs. Peel and press the garlic into a pan with heated oil and brown slightly.
2. Combine the wheatmeal and flour in a large mixing bowl, and then press a hollow down in the middle. Crumble the yeast into the hollow and sprinkle the sugar on top. Sprinkle the herb salt, herbs and pepper around the edges of the flour. Warm up the Kefir gently and pour over the yeast. Leave until the yeast has dissolved. Starting from the middle knead everything together into a smooth dough. Transfer the dough to a work surface and continue to knead well and then roll into a ball, cover and leave to rise at room temperature for 30–40 minutes, until the dough has doubled its original volume.
3. Knead the dough again, this time on a flour-covered work surface, and then roll again into a ball. Sprinkle some flour into a round rattan bread basket. Press the ball of dough into the basket, cover and leave to rise a further 30–40 minutes.
4. Cover a baking tray with grease-proof paper and turn the dough out

onto it carefully. Brush the bread dough with some milk and sprinkle coriander over the top. Press the seeds gently into the dough.
5. Bake in a preheated oven on the second shelf from the bottom. Pull off the baking tray with the paper. Leave to stand for at least 6–8 hours before slicing.

Baking time: approx. 50 minutes
Electric oven: 200° C

Gas oven: mark 3
Convection oven: 180° C

Per 100 g approx. 10 g P, 4 g L, 39 g G = 238 kcal (996 kj)

Tip
If you don't have a rattan basket, simply form the dough into a round loaf and bake straight on the baking tray.

Peanut Flat Bread Cakes

For 9 servings:
Dough:
350 g/12 oz plain wheat flour
150 g/5 oz whole grain rye meal
2 tsp salt
2 tsp sugar
30 g/1 oz yeast
125 ml/4½ fl oz lukewarm milk
125 ml/4½ fl oz lukewarm water
50 g/1¾ oz softened butter
Extras:
Flour, for preparation
Lard, to grease baking tray
Milk, for brushing
30 g/1 oz unsalted chopped peanuts

1. Combine the meal and flour in a mixing bowl. Press a hollow down into the middle and sprinkle the salt and sugar around the edges.

2. Crumble the yeast into the hollow. Pour the milk in the middle, add a little flour to it and then stir everything into a pre-dough. Cover and leave to rise for approx. 30 minutes.

3. Add the water and butter. Knead everything into a smooth dough. Cover and again leave the dough to rise, this time to double its original volume.

4. Knead the dough again and then separate into 9 equal portions. Roll each portion into a ball and then press down onto a flour-covered work surface into small flat bread loaves.

5. Lay the flat breads on a greased baking tray, brush over with the milk and sprinkle the peanuts on top. Cover and leave the dough to rise for the last time for approx. 15 minutes.

6. Bake in a preheated oven on the middle shelf.

Baking time: approx. 20 minutes
Electric oven: 200° C
Gas oven: mark 3
Convection oven: 180° C

Per piece approx. 7 g P, 6 g L, 37 g G = 247 kcal (1 040 kj)

Rustic Flat Bread

For 2 loaves:
Dough:
150 ml/¼ pint lukewarm milk
20 g/¾ oz yeast
250 g/9 oz plain wheat flour
A pinch of sugar • ½ tsp salt
20 g/¾ oz softened butter
125 g/4½ oz fried onions
Extras:
Flour, for preparation
Lard, to grease baking tray
1 tbsp milk, for brushing
1 tsp caraway seeds
1 tsp poppy seeds
1 tsp linseeds

1. Combine the milk, yeast, flour, sugar, salt and butter as described in the basic recipe on pages 10–11 to make a white bread dough.
2. Knead the onions into the dough. Cover and leave the dough to rise to double its original volume.
3. Separate the dough into 2 portions and form them on a flour-covered work surface into flat round bread loaves about 20–25 cm/ 8–10 in in diameter.
4. Place the loaves onto a greased baking tray and leave to rise for another 20 minutes.
5. Brush the loaves with some milk and then sprinkle the linseeds, caraway and poppy seeds over the top.
6. Bake in a preheated oven on the middle shelf.

Baking time: 30–35 minutes
Electric oven: 200° C
Gas oven: mark 3
Convection oven: 180° C

Per 100 g 7 g P, 12 g L, 32 g G = 286 kcal (1 201 kj)

Sunflower Bread

For 1 loaf:
Dough:
170 g/5 $^1/_2$ oz sunflower seeds
42 g/1 $^1/_2$ oz yeast • 2 tsp sea salt
300 ml/10 $^1/_2$ fl oz water
350 g/12 oz wholemeal wheat flour
2 tsp ground caraway
1 tbsp ground coriander
6 tbsp sunflower oil
150 g/5 oz wholemeal rye flour
Extras:
Lard, to grease baking tray
1 egg yolk

1. Dry roast 150 g/5 oz sunflower seeds in a frying pan. Dissolve the yeast and salt in a mixing bowl filled with the water. Add the wheat flour and flavourings stirring well and work into the dough for 5–10 minutes. Add 5 tablespoons of oil and the rye flour. Knead well until the dough forms a single mass and doesn't stick to the sides of the mixing bowl. Knead in the sunflower seeds. Roll the dough into a ball, cover and leave to rise at a temperature of around 18° C.
2. Knead the dough well once again. Place the loaves onto a greased baking tray, press down flat and leave to rise for another 20 minutes.
3. Take a pie cutting ring (7 $^1/_2$ cm/ 3 in diameter), make it wet and then press into the centre of the loaf. Make 7–8 long cuts towards the middle of the loaf from the outer edge using a sharp wet knife.
4. Whisk the egg yolk together with 1 tsp water and the rest of the sunflower oil and then brush onto the bread. Make sure, however, that you do not brush over the cuts. Sprinkle the rest of the sunflower seeds onto the marked circle in the middle. Place a fire-proof cup with cold water onto the floor of the oven. Bake the bread in a preheated oven on the second shelf from the bottom.

Baking time: approx. 40 minutes
Electric oven: 200° C
Gas oven: mark 3
Convection oven: 180° C

Per 100 g approx. 14 g P, 17 g L, 44 g G = 400 kcal (1 680 kj)

Seasoned Bread

For 2 loaves:
Dough:
1 tsp fennel seeds
600 g/1 lb 5 oz wholemeal wheat
flour
400 g/14 oz wholemeal rye flour
2 tbsp salt
1 tbsp ground coriander
2 tbsp caraway seeds
2 tsp ground aniseed
80 g/2¾ oz yeast
650 ml/1 pint 3 fl oz warm water
Extras:
Flour, for preparation
Lard, to grease baking tray

1. Grind down the fennel seeds finely using a mortar.
2. Mix both of the flours with the fennel, salt and the remaining seasoning in a bowl.
3. Crumble the yeast into the water and stir, then add to the flour mix and knead everything together into a smooth dough.
4. Cover and leave the dough to rise to double its original volume.
5. Knead the dough again and then separate into 2 equal portions. Form each portion into a long loaf shape on a flour-covered work surface and then lay on a greased baking tray.
6. Leave the dough to rise for the last time for approx. 20 minutes. Cut crosses into the top of each loaf and bake in a preheated oven on the middle shelf. Brush occasionally with water.

Baking time: approx. 1 hour
Electric oven: 200–225° C
Gas oven: mark 3–4
Convection oven: 180–200° C

Per 100 g approx. 10 g P, 2 g L, 56 g G =
306 kcal (1 286 kj)

Party Bread

For 1 loaf:
Dough:
250 ml/9 fl oz milk
60 g/2 oz butter
500 g/1 lb 2 oz plain wheat flour
42 g/1 1/2 oz (1 cube) yeast
1 tbsp sugar
1 tbsp salt
Filling:
150 g/5 oz Emmentaler cheese
125 g/4 1/2 oz brie cheese
200 g/7 oz feta cheese
150 g/5 oz cheese slices
1 egg
Extras:
Flour, for preparation
1 tbsp water
2 tbsp sunflower seeds

1. Heat the milk up gently and melt the butter in it. Add the flour to a mixing bowl and press down a hollow in the middle. Pour the lukewarm butter-milk into the hollow and then dissolve the yeast in it. Add the sugar and salt and knead everything into a smooth dough. Leave to rise in a warm place for approx. 1 hour.
2. To make the filling combine the brie, feta and sliced cheese in a mixing bowl and break down with a blender, grate the Emmental cheese into it and add the egg. Work everything into a creamy mass and leave to stand in a cool place.
3. Knead the dough well and then roll out on a flour-covered work surface into a 40 cm/16 in sided square. Pour over with the cheese

mass. Fold in each corner of the dough square toward the centre. Brush over with some water and then sprinkle sunflower seeds over the top, pushing them gently into the dough.
4. Place the bread on a baking tray covered with greaseproof paper and bake on the middle shelf of the oven (no need to preheat). Leave the bread to cool a little and then serve warm.

Baking time: 1 hour
Electric oven: 175° C
Gas oven: mark 3–4
Convection oven: not advisable

Per 100 g approx. 12 g P, 14 g L, 23 g G = 286 kcal (1 203 kj)

Herb Ring

For 1 ring loaf:
Dough:
40 g/1^1/$_2$ oz yeast
1 tsp sugar
250 ml/9 fl oz lukewarm water
500 g/1 lb 2 oz plain wheat flour
1 tsp salt • 2 tbsp oil
400 g/14 oz raw ham
300 g/10^1/$_2$ oz onions
4 bunches of mixed herbs (chervil,
basil, chives, rosemary, thyme)
100 g/3^1/$_2$ oz pumpkin seeds

Extras:
1 egg yolk • 3 tbsp milk

1. Combine the yeast with the sugar and lukewarm water and stir well, then leave to rise for 15 minutes.
2. Add the flour, salt and oil to the yeast and knead together well. Cover and leave the dough to stand for approx. 30 minutes.
3. Chop the ham into small cubes. Peel the onions and also chop into cubes. Wash and dab the herbs dry and then chop up finely. Mix everything in with the pumpkin seeds.
4. Knead the herb mix well into the dough. Form the dough into a round loaf and make a hole in the middle to form a ring.

5. Place the herb ring onto a baking tray covered with greaseproof paper. Whisk the egg yolk and milk together and brush over the ring. Bake in a preheated oven on the middle shelf.

Baking time: approx. 30 minutes
Electric oven: 225° C
Gas oven: mark 4
Convection oven: 200° C

Per 100 g approx. 9 g P, 12 g L, 19 g G =
239 kcal (1004 kj)

Eberbach Cloister Bread

For 1 loaf:
Dough:
250 ml/9 fl oz milk
80 g/2¾ oz butter
500 g/1 lb 2 oz plain wheat flour
30 g/1 oz yeast
80 g/2¾ oz sugar
A pinch of salt
1 egg
300 g/10½ oz Pecorino
(Italian hard cheese)
100 g/3½ oz cooked ham
1 bunch of fresh coriander
Extras:
1 bay leaf

1. Gently heat up the milk. Melt the butter in a saucepan and leave to cool. Sift the flour into a mixing bowl and press down a hollow in the middle.

2. Crumble the yeast into the hollow, add 1 teaspoon sugar, the milk and some flour and stir together to make a pre-dough. Cover and leave the dough to rise for approx. 20 minutes.

3. Add the remaining sugar, salt, butter and egg and knead everything together into a smooth dough using the kneading hooks on a mixer. Cover and leave the dough to rise again in a warm place for 30–40 minutes until it has doubled its original volume.

4. Chop the cheese and ham into small cubes. Wash the coriander, shake dry and chop up finely.

5. Add the remaining ingredients to the dough and knead together and then form into a bread loaf. Leave the dough to rise for a further 10 minutes. Bake the bread in a preheated oven on the second shelf from the bottom. Serve the bread warm and garnished with a bay leaf.

Baking time: approx. 50 minutes
Electric oven: 200° C
Gas oven: mark 3
Convection oven: 180° C

Per 100 g approx. 14 g P, 12 g L, 29 g G = 304 kcal (1 276 kj)

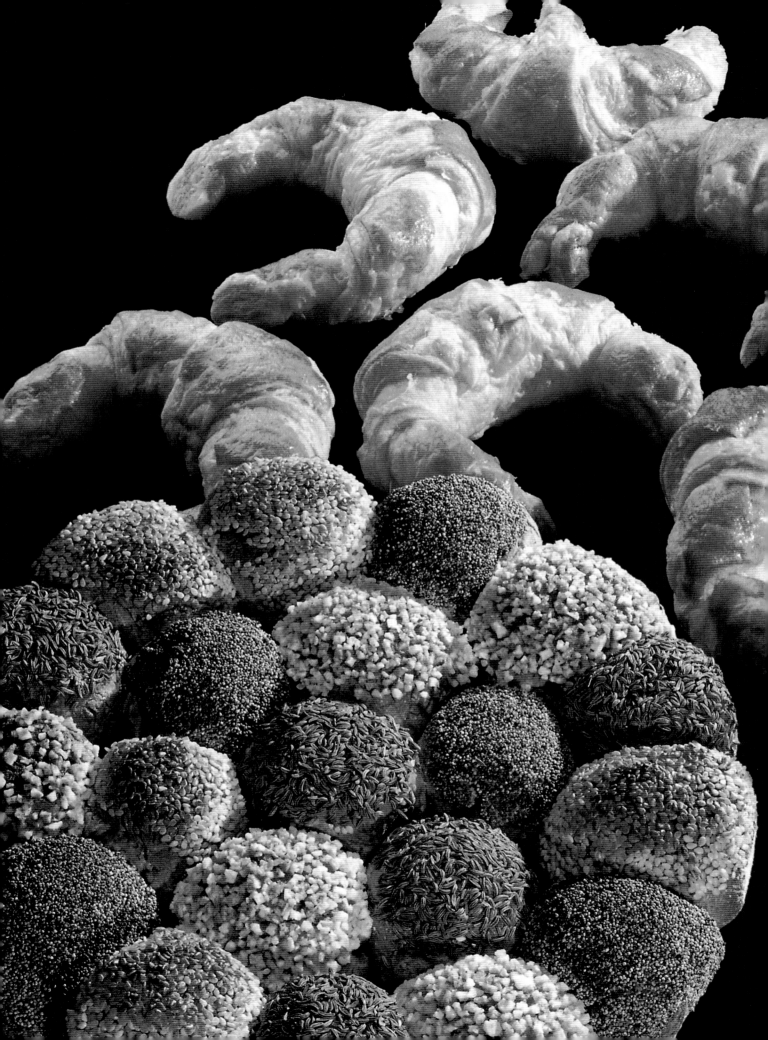

Crispy
Rolls

Roll Roses

For 16 rolls:
Dough:
330 g/11 oz wholemeal wheat flour
(very finely milled)
200 g/7 oz wheat flour
42 g/1$^1/_2$ oz (1 cube) yeast
1 tsp honey
300 ml/10$^1/_2$ fl oz lukewarm water
2 egg yolks • A pinch of sea salt
6 tbsp crème fraîche

Extras:
Flour, for preparation
Lard, to grease baking tray
2 egg yolks
2 tbsp whipping cream
1 tbsp poppy seeds

1. Add the flour to a mixing bowl and press down a hollow in the middle. Dissolve the yeast and honey in lukewarm water and pour into the hollow. Add the egg yolks, salt and crème fraîche to the edges of the flour. Starting from the middle knead everything together into a smooth dough. Cover and leave to rise in a warm place for approx. 20 minutes.

2. Sprinkle the dough with flour and knead again well. Roll the dough into a length and cut into 16 pieces. Roll each piece into a ball on a flour-covered work surface. Out of the small rolls make a large rose shape on a greased baking tray.

3. Whisk the egg yolk and cream together and brush over the rolls. Sprinkle over with the poppy seeds and leave once again to rise for 15 minutes.

4. Bake in a preheated oven on the middle shelf.

Baking time: 20–25 minutes
Electric oven: 200° C
Gas oven: mark 3
Convection oven: 180° C

Per roll approx. 6 g P, 5 g L, 22 g G = 160 kcal (665 kj)

Brioche

For 20 servings:
Dough:
500 g/1 lb 2 oz plain wheat flour
1 packet dried yeast
1 tbsp sugar
1 tsp salt
125 ml/4¹/₂ fl oz lukewarm milk
2 eggs
120 g/5 oz softened butter
Extras:
1 egg yolk

1. Sift the flour into a mixing bowl and mix with the yeast, sugar and salt.
2. Stir in the eggs, milk and butter. Knead everything into a smooth dough. Cover and leave the dough to rise to double its original volume.
3. Roll the dough into a length and cut into 20 equal portions. Roll a small ball and a large ball out of each portion.
4. Place the large dough balls in paper cake cups (5 cm/2 in diameter). Make an impression into the top of each dough ball and then press the smaller dough ball into it.

5. Whisk the egg yolk and brush over the brioche with it. Bake in a preheated oven on the middle shelf.

Baking time: approx. 20 minutes
Electric oven: 200° C
Gas oven: mark 3
Convection oven: 180° C

Per brioch approx. 4 g P, 6 g L, 16 g G = 149 kcal (628 kj)

Pumpkin Seed Rolls

For 12 rolls:
Dough:
300 g/10$^1/_2$ oz wholemeal wheat
flour (very finely milled)
200 g/5 oz wholegrain rye meal
1 tsp honey
42 g/1$^1/_2$ oz (1 cube) yeast
300 ml/10$^1/_2$ fl oz lukewarm water
50 g/1$^3/_4$ oz pumpkin seeds
Caraway seeds • A pinch of sea salt
50 g/1$^3/_4$ oz butter or margarine
Extras:
Wholemeal flour, for preparation

1. Combine the rye meal and flour in a large mixing bowl and then press a hollow down in the middle. Crumble the yeast and pour the honey into the lukewarm water, allow to dissolve and then pour into the hollow.

2. Chop up the pumpkin seeds finely (or mill coarsely), then add together with caraway seeds, salt and butter or margarine to the edges of the flour. Starting from the middle mix the ingredients and then knead everything into a smooth, elastic dough using the kneading hooks on a mixer. Cover and leave to rise in a warm place for 30–40 minutes.

3. Knead the dough again well on a flour-covered work surface. Roll the dough into a length and cut into 12 pieces. Roll each piece into a ball, dust over with some flour and place on a flour-covered baking tray. Cut a notch into the top of each roll. Leave the dough to rise for a further 15 minutes. Bake the rolls in a preheated oven on the second shelf from the bottom.

Baking time: 20–25 minutes
Electric oven: 200° C
Gas oven: mark 3
Convection oven: 180° C

Per roll approx. 8 g P, 6 g L, 28 g G = 206 kcal (863 kj)

Tip
Dry roast the pumpkin seeds in a frying pan. This lends the rolls a stronger aroma.

Sesame Croissants

For 12 croissants:
Dough:
300 g/10^1/$_2$ oz wheat flour
(finely milled)
200 g/7 oz oatmeal (finely milled)
15 g/^{1}/$_2$ oz ground mustard seeds
42 g/1^1/$_2$ oz (1 cube) yeast
1 tsp honey
300 ml/10^1/$_2$ fl oz lukewarm water
A pinch of sea salt
2 egg yolks
Extras:
Lard, to grease baking tray
Flour, to sprinkle
1 egg yolk
1 tsp water
4 tbsp shelled sesame seeds

1. Combine the wheat flour, oatmeal and ground mustard seeds. Add to a mixing bowl and press down a hollow in the middle. Dissolve the yeast and honey in lukewarm water and pour into the hollow, followed by the salt and egg yolk to the edges of the flour. Knead everything into a smooth dough using the kneading hooks on a mixer. Cover with cling film and leave to rise in a warm place for 30–40 minutes
2. Knead the dough once again. Roll the dough into a length and cut into 12 pieces. Form each piece into a croissant shape and then place on a greased and flour-dusted baking tray.
3. Stir the egg yolk together with the water. Brush onto the croissants and then sprinkle over with the sesame seeds. Leave the dough to rise for a further 15 minutes. Bake the croissants in a preheated oven on the middle shelf.

Baking time: approx. 25 minutes
Electric oven: 200° C
Gas oven: mark 3
Convection oven: 180° C

Per croissant approx. 7 g P, 4 g L, 25 g G = 171 kcal (713 kj)

Ring Rolls

For 12 rolls:
Dough:
40 g/1$^{1}/_{2}$ oz yeast
300 ml/10$^{1}/_{2}$ fl oz lukewarm water
300 g/10$^{1}/_{2}$ oz plain wheat flour
175 g/6 oz wholemeal wheat flour
50 g/1$^{3}/_{4}$ oz sugar
1 tsp salt
Extras:
Flour, for preparation
Lard, to grease baking tray
1 egg white
3 tbsp poppy seeds

1. Crumble the yeast into the water, stir into a paste and leave to rise for approx. 5 minutes.
2. Mix the flour with the sugar and salt and knead everything together into a smooth dough. Cover and leave the dough to rise to double its original volume.
3. Knead the dough again and then roll into one length. Cut into 12 equal portions.
4. Roll each portion into a ball and flatten slightly. Coat a finger in flour and use to press a large hole through the middle, making small rings. Place on a greased baking tray, cover and leave again to rise for approx. 10 minutes.
5. Brush the rings with egg white and sprinkle over with the poppy seeds. Bake in a preheated oven on the middle shelf.

Baking time: 20–25 minutes
Electric oven: 200° C
Gas oven: mark 3
Convection oven: 180° C

Per roll approx. 5 g P, 1 g L, 26 g G = 150 kcal (632 kj)

Emperor's Rolls

For 15 rolls:
Dough:
300 ml/10$^1/_2$ fl oz lukewarm milk
40 g/1$^1/_2$ oz yeast
500 g/1 lb 2 oz plain wheat flour
1 tsp sugar
1 tsp salt
75 g/2$^1/_2$ oz butter
Extras:
Flour, for preparation
Lard, to grease baking tray
1 egg yolk
1 egg

1. Combine the milk, yeast, flour, sugar, salt and butter as described in the basic recipe on pages 10–11 to make a white bread dough.
2. Roll the leavened dough into a thick length and cut into 15 equal portions. Roll each piece on a flour-covered work surface into 30 cm/12 in lengths.
3. Fold the rolled length in the middle to make two equal halves, but do not join them. Twist the strands around each other a few times and then thread the ends through the resulting loop at the bottom.

4. Place the twisted rolls onto a greased baking tray and leave to rise for another 15 minutes.
5. Whisk the egg and egg yolk together and brush over the rolls. Bake in a preheated oven on the middle shelf.

Baking time: 12–15 minutes
Electric oven: 200–225° C
Gas oven: mark 3–4
Convection oven: 180–200° C

Per Roll approx. 5 g P, 6 g L, 22 g G = 175 kcal (738 kj)

Hearty Party Rolls

For 16 rolls:
Dough:
300 g/10½ oz plain wheat flour
300 g/10½ oz wholemeal wheat flour
1 packet dried yeast
2 tsp salt
2 tsp coarsely ground pepper
½ l/18 fl oz lukewarm water
Extras:
Flour, for preparation
Lard, to grease baking tray

1. Mix both of the flours with the dried yeast, salt and 1 tablespoon pepper in a bowl.
2. Pour in the water and knead everything into a smooth dough. Cover and leave the dough to rise to double its original volume.
3. Separate the dough into 2 portions and roll them on a flour-covered work surface into a flat rectangle 20 x 40 cm/8 x 10 in. Brush some water over the dough and sprinkle over the rest of the pepper.
4. Roll the dough along its length and then cut into 5 cm/2 in pieces. Place the spiral dough rolls down flat onto a greased baking tray and leave to rise for another 10 minutes.

Bake in a preheated oven on the middle shelf.

Baking time: 20–25 minutes
Electric oven: 200° C
Gas oven: mark 3
Convection oven: 180° C

Per roll approx. 4 g P, 1 g L, 24 g G = 132 kcal (558 kj)

Cheesy Soda Rolls

For 16 rolls:
Dough:
500 g/1 lb 2 oz plain wheat flour
42 g/1½ oz (1 cube) yeast
1 tsp sugar
300 ml/10½ fl oz lukewarm water
1 tsp salt
150 g/5 oz goats Gouda cheese
150 g/5 oz Pecorino cheese
100 g/3½ oz crème fraîche
Freshly ground pepper
40 g/1½ oz bicarbonate of soda
Extras:
Flour, for preparation
Lard, to grease springform

1. Sift the flour into a mixing bowl and press down a hollow in the middle. Crumble the yeast and sprinkle the sugar into the hollow. Pour in 300 ml/10½ fl oz of warm water and dissolve the yeast in it. Sprinkle the salt over the flour and beginning from the middle knead everything into a smooth dough using the kneading hooks on a mixer.

2. Cover and leave the dough in a warm place for as long as it takes to rise to double its original volume. Knead well on a flour-covered work surface, until the dough is elastic and starts getting bubbly. Leave the dough to rise for a further 20 minutes.

3. Grate the Gouda and Pecorino cheeses while waiting. Then stir in the crème fraîche and season with the pepper.

4. Pour the rest of the water in a saucepan and dissolve the bicarbonate of soda in it. Bring the water to the boil and leave to cook for at least 10 minutes. Roll the dough out

flat on a flour-covered work surface into a 56 x 56 cm/22 x 22 in square and then cut into 16 smaller squares (14 x 14 cm/6 x 6 in).

5. Add a serving of the cheese mix to the middle of each square. Take the corners and fold them into the centre pressing down to make pastry shapes. Roll into balls. Dip the dough balls in the soda water for 1 minute using a draining spoon. Remove and leave on a cake tray to drip dry.

6. Grease a round baking tray (26 cm/10 in in diameter), pack with the dough balls pressing down on them slightly and leave to rise a little more.

7. Bake the soda rolls in a preheated oven on the second shelf from the bottom. Serve warm.

Baking time: approx. 30 minutes
Electric oven: 200° C
Gas oven: mark 3
Convection oven: 180° C

Per roll approx. 8 g P, 7 g L, 20 g G = 189 kcal (797 kj)

Bacon Rolls

For 16 rolls:
300 g/10½ oz small onions
150 g/5 oz streaky smoked bacon
250 g/9 oz wholegrain wheatmeal
250 g/9 oz wholemeal wheat flour
40 g/1½ oz yeast • Sugar
300 ml/10½ fl oz lukewarm water
10 g/⅓ oz salt
Flour, for preparation
Milk, for brushing

1. Peel the onions and thinly slice.
Chop the bacon into small cubes and
fry in a pan on medium heat until the
bacon begins to brown. Add the
onion slices and fry as well, turning
until both sides are golden brown.
Remove and place on a kitchen towel
to cool.
2. Combine the wheatmeal and
flour in a mixing bowl, press down
a hollow in the middle and then
crumble the yeast into it. Sprinkle
the sugar over the yeast, pour the
water in and allow to dissolve.
Sprinkle the salt onto the edges of
the flour. Starting from the middle,
knead everything together into a
smooth dough. Cover and leave the
dough in a warm place for as long as
it takes to rise to double its original
volume (30–40 minutes). Place the
dough on a flour-covered work
surface and knead in the onions and
bacon. Cover and leave the dough to
rise for another 10 minutes.
3. Roll the dough into a 40 cm/16 in
length and cut into 16 equal portions. Roll each portion into a ball
and then stretch into an oval shape.
4. Place the rolls on a baking tray
covered with greaseproof paper and
press down slightly. Leave covered
to rise for a further 8–10 minutes.
Then brush over with milk. Take a
sharp knife and make three diagonal
cuts into the top of each roll. Place
a cup of hot water into the oven and
then bake the rolls on the middle
shelf of a preheated oven.

Baking time: approx. 25 minutes
Electric oven: 200–225° C
Gas oven: mark 3–4
Convection oven: 180–200° C

Per Brötchen approx. 4 g P, 9 g L, 20 g G =
189 kcal (789 kj)

Rye Caraway Rolls

For 16 rolls:
Dough:
600 g/1 lb 5 oz wholemeal rye flour
50 g/1$^3/_4$ oz yeast
A sprinkling of sugar
10 g/$^1/_4$ oz salt
100 g/3$^1/_2$ oz softened pork fat
6 tsp caraway seeds
375 ml/13 fl oz water • 4 tbsp milk
Extras:
Flour, for preparation
Milk, for brushing
6 tsp caraway seeds and coarse salt,
to sprinkle

1. Add the flour to a mixing bowl
and press down a hollow in the
middle. Crumble the yeast into the
hollow and sprinkle the sugar on
top and then add the salt, fat and
caraway seeds around the edges of
the flour. Gently heat the water in a
saucepan and then pour over the
yeast. Leave until the yeast has
dissolved. Starting from the middle
knead everything together into a
smooth dough. Cover and leave the
dough in a warm place for as long
as it takes to rise to double its
original volume (30–40 minutes).
2. Roll the dough out onto a flour-
covered work surface into a 40 cm/
16 in length and cut into 16 equal
portions. Roll each portion into a
ball. Space the rolls apart on a
baking tray covered with greaseproof paper and press down slightly.
Cover and leave to rise for a further
10–15 minutes.
3. Brush each roll with the milk and
then make a lengthwise cut into the
top of each using a sharp knife.
Sprinkle the caraway seeds and
coarse salt over the top. Place a cup
of hot water into the oven and then
bake the rolls on the middle shelf of
a preheated oven.

Baking time:
approx. 25–35 minutes
Electric oven: 200˚ C
Gas oven: mark 3
Convection oven: 180˚ C

Per roll approx. 4 g P, 7 g L, 28 g G =
190 kcal (794 kj)

Ham Rolls

For 15 rolls:
Dough:
500 g/1 lb 2 oz plain wheat flour
1 packet dried yeast
1 tsp salt
250 ml/9 fl oz lukewarm water
1 egg
Extras:
150 g/5 oz raw ham
Flour, for preparation
Lard, to grease baking tray
Milk, for brushing

1. Combine the flour, salt and dried yeast.
2. Add the lukewarm water and egg. Knead everything into a smooth dough. Cover and leave the dough to rise to double its original volume.
3. Chop the ham into small cubes and then knead into the base of the dough mass.
4. Roll the leavened dough into a thick length and cut into 15 equal portions. Form the portions into long bread rolls and place on a greased baking tray. Cover and leave to rise for a further 10 minutes.
5. Brush the milk onto the tops of the rolls and then bake in a preheated oven on the middle shelf.

Baking time: approx. 20 minutes
Electric oven: 200° C
Gas oven: mark 3
Convection oven: 180° C

Per roll approx. 6 g P, 3 g L, 21 g G =
152 kcal (642 kj)

Onion Rolls

For 15 rolls:
Dough:
500 g/1 lb 2 oz plain wheat flour
1 packet dried yeast
1 tsp salt
250 ml/9 fl oz lukewarm water
1 egg
Extras:
125 g/4$\frac{1}{2}$ oz fried onions (ready-made)
Flour, for preparation
Lard, to grease baking tray
Milk, for brushing

1. Prepare the dough as described in the Ham Rolls recipe.
2. Knead the onions into the dough.
3. Stretch the rolls a little and leave to rise. Brush the rolls with the milk, make a slice along the top and bake.

Baking time: approx. 20 minutes
Electric oven: 200° C
Gas oven: mark 3
Convection oven: 180° C

Per roll approx. 4 g P, 3 g L, 23 g G =
157 kcal (659 kj)

Nutty Rolls

For 15 rolls:
Dough:
500 g/1 lb 2 oz plain wheat flour
1 packet dried yeast
1 tsp salt
250 ml/9 fl oz lukewarm water
1 egg
Extras:
200 g/7 oz walnuts
Flour, for preparation
Lard, to grease baking tray
Milk, for brushing

1. Prepare the dough as described in the Ham Rolls recipe.
2. Chop the walnuts up coarsely and knead into the base of the risen dough.
3. Stretch the rolls a little and leave to rise. Brush with the milk, cut a cross into the top and bake.

Poppy Seed Rolls

For 15 rolls:
Dough:
500 g/1 lb 2 oz plain wheat flour
1 packet dried yeast
1 tsp salt
250 ml/9 fl oz lukewarm water
1 egg
Extras:
Flour, for preparation
Lard, to grease baking tray
2 tbsp milk, for brushing
75 g/2¹/₂ oz poppy seeds

1. Prepare the dough as described in the Ham Rolls recipe, shaping and leaving to rise the same way too.
2. Brush the leavened rolls with the milk and sprinkle over with the poppy seeds.
3. Bake the poppy rolls in a preheated oven on the middle shelf.

Baking time: approx. 20 minutes
Electric oven: 200° C
Gas oven: mark 3
Convection oven: 180° C

Per roll approx. 5 g P, 4 g L, 22 g G =
164 kcal (692 kj)

Baking time: approx. 20 minutes
Electric oven: 200° C
Gas oven: mark 3
Convection oven: 180° C

Per roll approx. 5 g P, 3 g L, 22 g G =
152 kcal (640 kj)

Roll Cluster

For 20 rolls:
Dough:
375 g/13 oz wholemeal rye flour
375 g/13 oz whole grain rye meal
50 g/1 3/4 oz yeast
A pinch of sugar
1 tbsp salt
1/2 l/18 fl oz water
4 tbsp milk
3 tbsp oil

Extras:
Wholemeal rye flour
and wheatmeal, to sprinkle
Lard, to grease baking tray
1 egg white, for brushing
Poppy seeds, caraway seeds,
sesame seeds and coarse salt,
to sprinkle

1. Add the rye flour and rye meal to a mixing bowl and press down a hollow in the middle. Crumble the yeast into the hollow. Sprinkle over with the sugar and add the salt to the edges of the flour. Combine the water and milk, gently heat in a saucepan and then pour over the yeast. Leave until the yeast has dissolved. Knead everything into a smooth dough, while adding the oil slowly. Dust the rye flour onto the dough, cover and leave in a warm place to rise for 30–40 minutes.

2. Place the ring of a 28 cm/11 in round cake tray onto a baking tray. Grease the baking tray within the ring and then sprinkle over with the wheatmeal.

3. Roll the dough on a flour-covered work surface into a large ball and then separate into 2 portions, cover and leave to stand a further 10 minutes.

4. Roll each portion of dough into a 40 cm/16 in length and cut into 10 equal pieces. Cover to prevent a crust forming. Roll each piece into a

ball and place next to each other in the round tray starting with 13 rolls on the outside then 6 in the middle and finally the last one to close the middle. Brush the egg white onto all of them and then sprinkle 5 rolls each with poppy, caraway and sesame seeds or salt. Leave covered to rise for a further 15–20 minutes.

5. Place a cup of hot water on the bottom shelf of the oven. Remove the cake tray ring and then place the cluster in a preheated oven on the second shelf from the bottom and bake. Remove and place on a cake rack to cool.

Baking time: approx. 40 minutes
Electric oven: 200° C
Gas oven: mark 3
Convection oven: 180° C

Per roll approx. 4 g P, 2 g L, 23 g G = 136 kcal (570 kj)

Puff Pastry Croissants

For 20 croissants:
Dough:
2 packets of puff pastry
(each 300 g/10$\frac{1}{2}$ oz)
Filling:
100 g/3$\frac{1}{2}$ oz leek
(only the white parts)
10 g/$\frac{1}{3}$ oz butter or margarine
2 tbsp water
100 g/3$\frac{1}{2}$ oz cooked ham
100 g/3$\frac{1}{2}$ oz sheeps milk cheese
1 bunch of thyme
1 egg • 1 tbsp whipping cream
Freshly ground white pepper
Extras:
Flour, for preparation
Water, to brush • 1 egg yolk

1. Leave the puff pastry to defrost and then slice each piece diagonally in half. Roll each triangle out onto a lightly floured work surface to make a little larger.

2. While waiting for the puff pastry to completely defrost, trim and clean the leek and then slice lengthwise in half. Cut the leek into thin strips and finally small squares, and then fry gently in the butter or margarine with 2 tablespoons of water and leave to cool.

3. Chop the ham and cheese into small cubes. Pluck the thyme leaves from the stem and chop up, but not too finely. Mix the egg with the cream. Add everything to a mixing bowl, stir together and season with the pepper.

4. Add the prepared filling (1 level tablespoon) to the longer edge of the dough triangle. Brush water onto the top corner of the triangle. Roll the triangles together and form into croissant shapes, then place on a baking tray that has been rinsed in cold water. Brush the whisked egg yolk onto the tops of the rolls and then bake in a preheated oven on the middle shelf. Serve the croissants warm.

Baking time:
approx. 12–15 minutes
Electric oven: 225° C
Gas oven: mark 4
Convection oven: 200° C

Per Croissant approx. 4 g P, 12 g L, 9 g G = 167 kcal (701 kj)

Cheese Bakes

For approx. 40 servings:
Dough:
2 packets of puff pastry
(each 300 g/10$\frac{1}{2}$ oz)
Extras:
Milk, for brushing
300 g/10$\frac{1}{2}$ oz grated cheese

1. Leave the puff pastry to defrost according to the instructions on the packaging. Place the dough pieces on top of each other and then roll out into a 40 x 50 cm/16 x 20 in rectangle.
2. Brush the puff pastry with milk and sprinkle the cheese on top.
3. Take the shorter side of the rectangle and fold the pastry twice and then fold again in half along its length.
4. Cut the dough into slices (1 cm/$\frac{1}{3}$ in thick). Place the slices face upwards on a baking tray covered with greaseproof paper and then bake on the middle shelf of a preheated oven.
5. When ready remove the bakes from the paper and place on a cake rack to cool.

Baking time: 15–20 minutes
Electric oven: 200° C
Gas oven: mark 3
Convection oven: 180° C

Per serving approx. 2 g P, 6 g L, 4 g G = 94 kcal (397 kj)

Poppy Seed and Salt Sticks

For approx. 50 servings:
Dough:
300 ml/10½ fl oz lukewarm milk
40 g/1½ oz yeast
500 g/1 lb 2 oz plain wheat flour
1 tsp sugar
1 tsp salt
40 g/1½ oz softened butter
Extras:
Flour, for preparation
Lard, to grease baking tray
1 egg yolk
2 tbsp milk
75 g/2½ oz poppy seeds
2 tbsp coarse salt

1. Combine the milk, yeast, flour, sugar, salt and butter as described in the basic recipe on pages 10–11 to make a white bread dough.
2. Place the leavened dough on a flour-covered work surface and knead again, then roll into a 50 cm/20 in length and cut into 50 equal portions.
3. Roll each portion into a 12 cm/ 5 in stick and place onto a greased baking tray. Leave to rise once again for 10 minutes.
4. Whisk the egg yolk and milk together and brush over the sticks. Sprinkle poppy seeds on one half of the sticks and salt on the other.
5. Bake in a preheated oven on the middle shelf.

Baking time: approx. 20 minutes
Electric oven: 200° C
Gas oven: mark 3
Convection oven: 180° C

Per serving approx. 1 g P, 1 g L, 7 g G = 54 kcal (228 kj)

Parmesan Rings, Salt Pretzels, Caraway Sticks

For 30 servings:
Dough:
1 kg/2 lbs 3 oz plain wheat flour
42 g/1 $\frac{1}{2}$ oz (1 cube) yeast
375 ml/13 fl oz water
250 ml/9 fl oz milk
1 tsp sugar
1 tsp salt
50 g/1 $\frac{3}{4}$ oz butter or margarine
Extras:
Flour, for preparation
Parmesan Rings:
Water, for brushing
100 g/3 $\frac{1}{2}$ oz freshly grated
Parmesan cheese
1 egg white
Salt Pretzels:
1 tbsp milk, for brushing
2 tbsp coarse salt
Caraway Sticks:
1 tbsp milk
1 tbsp caraway seeds

1. Add the flour to a mixing bowl, press down a hollow in the middle and then crumble the yeast into it. Mix the water and milk together and heat up gently. Sprinkle the sugar over the yeast, pour the diluted milk into the hollow and allow the yeast to dissolve. Add the salt and softened butter or margarine to the edges of the flour and then, beginning from the middle, knead all the ingredients into a smooth dough. Cover and leave the dough at room temperature for as long as it takes to rise to double its original volume (30–40 minutes).
2. Knead the dough again well on a flour-covered work surface and then roll into a 30 cm/12 in length. Separate into 3 equal portions. Roll each portion into a ball.
3. To make the Parmesan Rings: roll a ball of dough out flat on a flour-covered work surface. (Cover the other two dough balls, and place somewhere cool so that they do not continue to rise). Leave the rolled out sheet of dough to rise for approximately 5 minutes. Brush a little water over the top and then sprinkle with 50 g/1 $\frac{3}{4}$ oz of the freshly grated Parmesan cheese. Cut the sheet of dough into 10

(40 cm/16 in long) strips. Take each strip and twist into a long spiral. Join the ends and pinch them together to make a ring. Whisk the egg white gently and then brush the rings with it. Take each egg-coated ring and drag through the remaining Parmesan cheese and then place on a baking tray covered with greaseproof paper. Cover and leave to rise for 10 minutes. Bake in a preheated oven on the second shelf from the bottom.
4. To make the Salt Pretzels: take a second dough ball, place on the flour-covered work surface and roll into a 50 cm/20 in length. Cut the length into 10 equal portions. Roll each piece between the hands into a 40 cm/16 in length and loop into a Pretzel shape. Place the Pretzels onto a baking tray covered with greaseproof paper, cover and leave to rise for 10 minutes. Brush the dough with some milk and sprinkle salt over the top. Bake in a preheated oven on the second shelf from the bottom.
5. To make the Caraway Sticks: roll the last dough ball on a flour-covered work surface into a 50 cm/20 in length. Cut the length into 10 equal portions. Roll each portion between the hands into 30 cm/12 in stick lengths. Place the sticks about 2 cm/$\frac{3}{4}$ in apart on a baking tray covered with greaseproof paper. Pinch each end down with the thumb. Cover and leave to rise for approximately 10 minutes. Brush over with the milk and then sprinkle with the caraway seeds. Bake in a preheated oven on the second shelf from the bottom.
6. Remove from the baking tray as soon as the sticks are ready baked and leave to cool.

Baking time:
approx. 20–25 minutes
Electric oven: 200° C
Gas oven: mark 3
Convection oven: 180° C

Per serving approx. 6 g P, 3 g L, 24 g G =
151 kcal (630 kj)

Herb Rolls

For 15 rolls:
Dough:
500 g/1 lb 2 oz plain wheat flour
1 packet dried yeast
1 tsp salt
250 ml/9 fl oz lukewarm water
1 egg
Extras:
1 bunches of chives
1 tbsp chopped parsley
1 tbsp chopped dill
Flour, for preparation
Lard, to grease baking tray
Milk, for brushing

1. Combine the flour, salt and dried yeast.

2. Add the lukewarm water and egg. Knead everything into a smooth dough. Cover and leave the dough to rise to double its original volume.

3. While waiting wash the chives, shake dry and chop up into small rolls.

4. Knead the dough again, adding the chive rings and remaining herbs. Roll the leavened dough on a flour-covered work surface into a thick length and cut into 15 equal portions. Form the portions into bread roll shapes and place on a greased baking tray. Cover and leave to rise for a further 10 minutes.

5. Brush the milk onto the tops of the rolls and then bake in a pre-heated oven on the middle shelf.

Baking time: approx. 20 minutes
Electric oven: 200˚ C
Gas oven: mark 3
Convection oven: 180˚ C

Per roll approx. 4 g P, 1 g L, 21 g G = 123 kcal (517 kj)

Whole Grain Rolls

For 16 rolls:
Dough:
500 g/1 lb 2 oz wholemeal
wheat flour • 2 tsp salt
300 ml/10½ fl oz wheat beer
40 g/1½ oz yeast
150 g/5 oz sunflower seeds
Extras:
Flour, for preparation
Lard, to grease baking tray
Milk, for brushing

1. Combine the flour and salt in a mixing bowl.
2. Heat the beer up gently, crumble in the yeast and stir well. Pour over the flour and knead everything into a smooth dough, adding the sunflower seeds when the dough is elastic. Cover and leave the dough to rise to double its original volume.
3. Knead the dough again on a flour-covered work surface and roll into a thick length, then cut into 16 equal portions and form these into bread roll shapes.
4. Place the rolls onto a greased baking tray and leave to rise for another 15 minutes, then brush over with the milk. Bake in a preheated oven on the middle shelf.

Baking time: approx. 20 minutes
Electric oven: 200° C
Gas oven: mark 3
Convection oven: 180° C

Per roll approx. 6 g P, 0,4 g L, 17 g G = 110 kcal (463 kj)

Sweet Temptations

Amsterdam White Bread

For 1 loaf:
Dough:
500 g/1 lb 2 oz plain wheat flour
250 ml/9 fl oz milk
40 g/1 1/2 oz yeast
60 g/2 oz sugar
A pinch of salt
1 egg
100 g/3 1/2 oz butter
Extras:
Flour, for preparation
Lard, to grease baking tray
1 egg yolk
1 egg
2 tbsp caster sugar

1. Combine the flour, milk, yeast, sugar, salt, egg and butter, as described in the basic recipe on pages 10–11, to make a yeast dough.
2. Place the leavened dough on a flour-covered work surface and form into a loaf of approx. 40 cm/16 in length.
3. Then take some kitchen scissors and make a cut 10 cm/4 in inwards at both ends.
4. Take each of the 4 strands and spiral them inwards toward the loaf, one above and one below the other. Then press the spirals down firmly into the top and bottom edges of the loaf.
5. Place the loaf onto a greased baking tray and leave to rise for another 15 minutes.

6. Whisk the egg and egg yolk together and brush over the bread.
7. Bake in a preheated oven on the middle shelf. Brush periodically with the whisked egg.
8. Once ready baked allow the loaf to cool and then sprinkle some castor sugar on top.

Baking time: 40–50 minutes
Electric oven: 180° C
Gas oven: mark 2
Convection oven: 160° C

Per 100 g approx. 7 g P, 11 g L, 37 g G = 292 kcal (1 227 kj)

Fitness Bread

For 1 loaf:
Dough:
350 g/12 oz plain wheat flour
1 packet dried yeast
1 tsp salt
1 tsp sugar
50 g/1$\frac{3}{4}$ oz softened butter
125 ml/4$\frac{1}{2}$ fl oz lukewarm milk
1 egg
250 g/9 oz mixed baking fruit
2 tbsp chopped hazelnuts
1 tbsp chopped walnuts
1 tbsp chopped almonds
Extras:
Lard, to grease bread tin

1. Combine the yeast, sugar and salt. Add the butter, milk and egg and then knead everything into a smooth dough. Cover and leave the dough to rise to double its original volume.
2. Chop the baking fruit up into small cubes and fold into the dough together with the chopped hazelnuts, walnuts and almonds and continue to knead.
3. Place the ready dough into a greased bread tin (25 cm/9 in long), cover and leave to rise for a further 20 minutes.
4. Bake in a preheated oven on the middle shelf. Brush occasionally with water to prevent the dough from drying out.

Baking time: approx. 40 minutes
Electric oven: 175–200° C
Gas oven: mark 2–3
Convection oven: 150–180° C

Per 100 g approx. 7 g P, 11 g L, 31 g G =
271 kcal (1 140 kj)

Plaited Muesli Loaf

For 1 plaited loaf:
Dough:
150 g/5 oz low fat quark
75 g/2½ oz sugar
1 egg • A pinch of salt
6 tbsp oil
250 g/9 oz plain wheat flour
2 tsp baking powder
75 g/2½ oz currants
75 g/2½ oz raisins
75 g/2½ oz almond pieces
75 g/2½ oz chopped hazelnuts
Extras:
Flour, for preparation
1 egg yolk • 2 tbsp milk
100 g/3½ oz caster sugar
1 egg white

1. Add the quark to a mixing bowl.
Add the sugar, egg and salt and stir
together.
2. Stir in the oil gradually until a
smooth paste results.
3. Combine the flour with the
baking powder, fold into the quark
batter and then knead.
4. Combine the currants, raisins,
almond pieces and nuts, fold into
the dough and then knead well.
Cover and leave to stand for
10 minutes.
5. Separate the dough into
3 portions and form them, on a
flour-covered work surface, into
25 cm/8 in lengths. Plait the
3 lengths together and then place
onto a baking tray covered with
greaseproof paper.
6. Whisk the egg yolk and milk
together. Brush over the plaited loaf
and then bake in a preheated oven
on the middle shelf. Remove the
plaited loaf and leave to cool on a
cake rack.
7. Stir the egg white and castor
sugar into a smooth paste and
brush over the muesli loaf before
serving.

Baking time: 25–30 minutes
Electric oven: 200° C
Gas oven: mark 3
Convection oven: 180° C

Per 100 g approx. 7 g P, 23 g L, 37 g G =
400 kcal (1 681 kj)

Spicy Bread with Soured Milk

For 1 loaf:
Dough:
125 ml/4 $^1/_2$ fl oz lukewarm milk
40 g/1 $^1/_2$ oz yeast
500 g/1 lb 2 oz plain wheat flour
60 g/2 oz sugar
A pinch of salt • 1 egg
100 g/3 $^1/_2$ oz butter
150 g/5 oz soured milk
1 tsp grated rind of
an untreated orange
1 tsp ground aniseed
1 tsp ground cloves
125 g/4 $^1/_2$ oz rum raisins
50 g/1 $^3/_4$ oz chopped hazelnuts
40 g/1 $^1/_2$ oz chopped pine nuts
Extras:
Lard, to grease bread tin
1 egg yolk • 1 tbsp honey

1. Combine the milk, yeast, flour, sugar, salt, egg and butter, as described in the basic recipe on pages 10–11, and make a yeast dough, also adding the soured milk, orange peel, aniseed and cloves together with the butter and egg to the edges of the flour. Starting from the middle knead everything together into a smooth dough.
2. Fold in the raisins, nuts and pine nuts and knead well. Cover and leave the dough to rise to double its original volume.
3. Place the ready dough into a greased bread tin (30 cm/12 in long), cover and leave to rise for a further 20 minutes.
4. Whisk the egg yolk and brush over the bread. Bake in a preheated oven on the second shelf from the bottom.
5. Remove and leave to cool a little, knock out of the bread tin and serve warm and spread with honey.

Baking time: approx. 45 minutes
Electric oven: 200˚ C
Gas oven: mark 3
Convection oven: 180˚ C

Per 100 g approx. 7 g P, 12 g L, 37 g G = 300 kcal (1 263 kj)

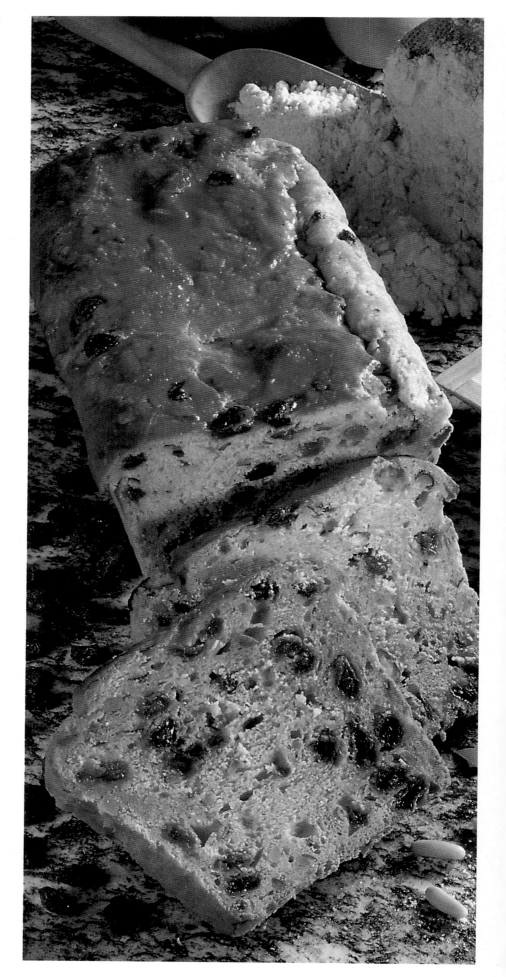

Banana Bread

For 1 loaf:
Dough:
225 g/9 oz plain wheat flour
2 tsp baking powder
A pinch of salt
175 g/6 oz brown sugar
1 tsp grated rind of an
untreated orange
1 tsp grated rind of an
untreated lemon
75 g/7 oz raisins
120 g/5 oz butter or margarine
2 ripe bananas
1 tbsp lemon juice
1 egg
2 tbsp orange juice
Extras:
Lard, to grease bread tin
1 tbsp runny honey
1 banana
A few drops of lemon juice
Fresh peppermint leaves, to garnish
Orange peel strips

1. Sift the flour into a mixing bowl and combine with the baking powder. Add to it the salt, sugar, fruit peel and raisins.
2. Work the butter or margarine into the ingredients until everything becomes crumbly.
3. Peel the banana and press down into a paste, adding the lemon juice. Whisk the egg. Work the banana, egg and orange juice into the flour mix.
4. Spoon the creamy dough mix into a greased and flour-dusted bread tin (1 1/2 pints 13 fl oz).
5. Bake the bread in a preheated oven on the second shelf from the bottom, until the loaf is firm to the touch. Leave to cool in the bread tin.
6. Knock the bread out of the tin and then spread honey over the top. Peel the banana and cut into slices, then dribble with the lemon juice. Decorate the banana loaf with the banana slices, peppermint leaves and orange peel and serve.

Baking time:
approx. 1 hour 10 minutes
Electric oven: 180° C
Gas oven: mark 2
Convection oven: 160° C

Per 100 g approx. 3 g P, 9 g L, 39 g G = 272 kcal (1 143 kj)

Franzi Rolls

For 20 rolls:
Dough:
500 g/9 oz plain wheat flour
42 g/1 1/2 oz (1 cube) yeast
70 g/3/4 oz sugar
125 ml/4 1/2 fl oz lukewarm milk
70 g/2 3/4 oz butter or margarine
A pinch of salt
1 tsp grated rind of an
untreated lemon
Dough filling:
200 g/9 oz butter
2 tsp cinnamon powder
200 g/3/4 oz sugar
Extras:
Flour, for preparation
Lard, to grease the baking tray

1. Add the flour to a mixing bowl, press down a hollow in the middle and then crumble the yeast into it. Sprinkle some sugar over the top and then pour the milk in to dissolve the yeast. Add the butter or margarine, remaining sugar, salt and lemon peel to the edges of the flour. Starting from the middle mix the ingredients using the kneading hooks on a mixer or by hand, and knead into a smooth, elastic dough. Cover and leave the dough in a warm place for as long as it takes to rise to double its original volume (30–40 minutes).

2. Knead the dough well once again. Roll the dough on a flour-covered work surface into a 25 x 30 cm/ 10 x 12 in rectangle.

3. Cut the cooled butter into thin slices and place onto one half of the dough. Fold the dough in half over the butter. Pinch the edges of the dough together and fold them under. Roll the dough out again on a flour-covered work surface into a 30 x 50 cm/12 x 20 in rectangle. Take the shorter side of the rectangle and fold it 1/3 inwards, then flap the other side over to create 3 layers. Leave to stand in a cool place for 15 minutes.

4. Roll the dough out once again on a flour-covered work surface into a 40 x 80 cm/16 x 32 in rectangle. Brush over with water. Mix the cinnamon and sugar, and sprinkle evenly over the dough.

5. Roll the flat dough up starting from the longer side into a 6 cm/2 1/3 in wide, slightly flattened length. The end edge of the dough should be on the underside of the long roll. Slice the dough roll into 4 cm/1 1/2 in wide portions. Press the top of each portion down toward the work surface using a wooden spoon. Spread out on two greased baking trays at least 4 cm/1 1/2 in apart and then cover up. Place the baking trays with the Franzi rolls in a warm place to rise for 15–10 minutes. Move the trays to somewhere cool to slow down the rising process of the dough. Bake in a preheated oven on the middle shelf.

Baking time: approx. 25 minutes
Electric oven: 200˚ C
Gas oven: mark 3
Convection oven: 180˚ C

Per roll approx. 3 g P, 11 g L, 33 g G = 247 kcal (1 031 kj)

Raisin Rolls

For 16 rolls:
Dough:
500 g/9 oz plain wheat flour
50 g/^{3}/$_4$ oz sugar
1 tsp salt
40 g/^{3}/$_4$ yeast
200 ml/14 fl oz lukewarm water
50 g/^{3}/$_4$ oz softened butter
1 egg
200 g/7 oz raisins
Extras:
Flour, for preparation
Milk, for brushing

1. Sift the flour into a mixing bowl. Sprinkle the sugar and salt on top.
2. Crumble the yeast into the water and stir to dissolve it, and then add to the flour together with the butter and egg. Knead everything into a smooth dough, folding the raisins in at the end. Cover and leave the dough to rise to double its original volume.
3. Knead the dough again on a flour-covered work surface and roll into a thick length, then cut into 16 equal portions and form these into bread roll shapes.
4. Place the rolls onto a baking tray covered with greaseproof paper, cover and leave to rise for 10 minutes. Brush over with some

milk and then bake in a preheated oven on the middle shelf.

Baking time: approx. 20 minutes
Electric oven: 200° C
Gas oven: mark 3
Convection oven: 180° C

Per roll approx. 4 g P, 3 g L, 31 g G = 184 kcal (773 kj)

73

Sweet Ring 'o' Rolls

For 15 rolls:
Dough:
200 ml/$^1/_4$ pint milk
40 g/$^3/_4$ yeast
500 g/9 oz plain wheat flour
80 g/$^3/_4$ oz sugar
1 tsp salt
80 g/$^3/_4$ oz softened butter
1 egg
Extras:
Flour, for preparation
Lard, to grease baking tray
1 egg white
50 g/1$^3/_4$ oz poppy seeds
50 g/1$^3/_4$ oz sesame seeds
50 g/1$^3/_4$ oz decorating sugar

1. Combine the milk, yeast, flour, sugar, salt and butter as described in the basic recipe on pages 10–11 to make a white bread dough. Fold in the egg and knead well.
2. Roll the leavened dough on a flour-covered work surface into one thick length and cut into 15 equal portions. Roll each portion into a ball. Pack the dough balls close together on a greased baking tray. Leave to rise once again for 15 minutes.
3. Brush over with some egg white. Sprinkle 5 rolls each with the poppy seeds, sesame seeds and decorating sugar. Bake in a preheated oven on the middle shelf.

Baking time: 20–25 minutes
Electric oven: 200° C
Gas oven: mark 3
Convection oven: 180° C

Per rolls approx. 6 g P, 9 g L, 31 g G = 243 kcal (1 022 kj)

Sunday Croissants

For 15 croissants:
Dough:
150 ml/^{1}/$_4$ pint lukewarm milk
25 g/^{3}/$_4$ yeast
400 g/9 oz plain wheat flour
50 g/^{3}/$_4$ oz sugar
A pinch of salt
200 g/^{3}/$_4$ oz softened butter
Extras:
Flour, for preparation
Lard, to grease baking tray
1 egg yolk
1 tbsp milk

1. Combine the milk, yeast, flour, sugar, salt and butter as described in the basic recipe on pages 10–11 to make a white bread dough.
2. Roll the leavened dough on a flour-covered work surface until it is about ^{1}/$_2$ cm/^{1}/$_4$ in thick. Cut 15 equally sized triangles out of the dough using a cutting wheel.
3. Roll the dough up from the base of the triangle and then shape into croissants.
4. Place the croissants onto a greased baking tray and leave to rise for another 10 minutes.
5. Whisk the egg yolk and milk together and brush over the croissants. Bake in a preheated oven on the middle shelf.

Baking time: 10–15 minutes
Electric oven: 200° C
Gas oven: mark 3
Convection oven: 180° C

Per croissant approx. 3 g P, 12 g L, 21 g G = 173 kcal (726 kj)

Pressburg Croissants

For 16 croissants:

Nut filling:
6 tbsp milk
1 stem of vanilla • 1 tbsp yeast
A sprinkling of pimento
75 g/2$\frac{1}{2}$ oz ground walnuts
25 g/1 oz chopped up raisins

Poppy seed filling:
6 tbsp whipping cream • 1 tbsp sugar
A sprinkling of pimento
75 g/2$\frac{1}{2}$ oz poppy seeds
25 g/1 oz chopped up raisins
1 tbsp rum

Dough:
375 g/9 oz plain wheat flour
20 g/$\frac{3}{4}$ oz yeast • 1 tsp sugar
200 ml/$\frac{1}{4}$ pint lukewarm milk
2 egg yolks
80 g/2$\frac{3}{4}$ oz butter or margarine
A pinch of salt

Extras:
Flour, for preparation
Lard, to grease baking tray
1 egg yolk • 1 tbsp milk
30 g/1 oz caster sugar, to decorate

1. To make the nut filling stir the milk together with the vanilla extract, sugar and pimento. Bring the milk to the boil, stir in the nuts and then remove from the heat. Stir in the raisins and leave to cool.

2. To make the poppy seed filling, heat up the cream, stirring in the sugar and pimento. Bring briefly to the boil, stir in the poppy seeds and then remove from the heat. Stir in the rum and raisins and leave to cool.

3. Add the flour to a mixing bowl, press down a hollow in the middle and then crumble the yeast into it. Sprinkle the sugar over the top and then pour the milk in to dissolve the yeast. Add the butter or margarine, salt and egg yolk to the edges of the flour. Starting from the middle knead everything together into a smooth dough. Cover and leave the dough at room temperature for as long as it takes to rise to double its original volume (30–40 minutes).

4. Knead the dough again well and roll out on a lightly floured work surface into a rectangle (40 x 50 cm/16 x 20 in), cutting the edges to make them straight. Cut the rolled dough into 8 squares each 12$\frac{1}{2}$ x 20 cm/5 x 8 in. Slice the squares diagonally in half to make 2 triangles. Make a 2 cm/$\frac{3}{4}$ in cut in the middle of the shorter edge of each triangle (opposite the pointed top) and then brush over with water. Spoon 2 teaspoons of the nut filling onto 8 triangles and 2 teaspoons of the poppy seed filling to the other 8 triangles. Pull each dough triangle slightly apart away from the cut and then roll into croissant shapes.

5. Place the croissants onto a greased baking tray and leave to rise for another 10 minutes. Stir the egg yolk and milk together and brush over the croissants. Bake in a preheated oven on the middle shelf until golden brown. Leave to cool on a cake rack, dust over with caster sugar and serve.

Baking time: 15–20 minutes
Electric oven: 200° C
Gas oven: mark 3
Convection oven: 180° C

Per croissant with nut filling approx.
6 g P, 13 g L, 26 g G = 252 kcal (1058 kj)

Per croissant with poppy seed filling approx.
6 g P, 13 g L, 29 g G = 271 kcal (1134 kj)

Chocolate Croissants

For 16 croissants:
Dough:
2 packets of frozen puff pastry
(each 300 g/10$^1/_2$ oz)
Filling:
200 g/7 oz dark chocolate
125 g/4$^1/_2$ oz sugar brittle
Extras:
Flour, for preparation
1 egg yolk
2 tbsp milk
100 g/3$^1/_2$ oz dark chocolate coating

1. Leave the puff pastry to defrost according to the instructions on the packaging.
2. Place the dough pieces on a lightly floured work surface and then roll together into a 40 x 50 cm/16 x 20 in rectangle.
3. Cut the rolled dough into 8 squares each 12$^1/_2$ x 20 cm/5 x 8 in. Slice the squares diagonally in half to make 2 triangles.
4. Break the chocolate up into small pieces and then add to the base edge of each triangle. Sprinkle the brittle on top.
5. Whisk the egg yolk and milk together and brush over the edges of the dough triangles.
6. Roll the dough up starting from the wider edge and then shape into croissants, then place on a baking tray covered with greaseproof paper.
7. Bake the croissants in a preheated oven on the middle shelf. Remove when golden brown and leave to cool on a cake rack.
8. Melt the dark chocolate coating and pour into a small icing bag with a fine nozzle attachment. Decorate the croissants with fine threads of chocolate, leave to dry and serve.

Baking time: approx. 25 minutes
Electric oven: 200° C
Gas oven: mark 3
Convection oven: 180° C

Per croissant approx. 3 g P, 18 g L, 27 g G = 300 kcal (1 261 kj)

Marzipan Croissants

For 8 croissants:
Dough:
300g/9 oz plain wheat flour
Salt
20 g/³/₄ oz sugar
20 g/³/₄ yeast
125 ml/4¹/₂ fl oz milk
20 g/9 oz butter
1 egg
Filling:
100 g/3¹/₂ oz fresh marzipan
100 g/3¹/₂ oz cooking chocolate
Extras:
Flour, for preparation
Lard, to grease baking tray
1 tbsp caster sugar

1. Combine the milk, yeast, flour, sugar, salt, egg and butter, as described in the basic recipe on pages 10–11, to make a yeast dough.
2. To make the filling, break up the fresh marzipan and the cooking chocolate into small pieces and knead them both together.
3. Place the dough on a flour-covered work surface and then roll into a 24 x 48 cm/9¹/₂ x 19 in rectangle. Cut out into 8 squares (12 x 12 cm/4³/₄ x 4³/₄ in).
4. Pour the filling over the squares, cleaning up the edges with a kitchen towel, then fold over from one edge to make a loose roll, and finally shape into croissants and then place on a greased baking tray.
5. Bake in a preheated oven on the second shelf from the bottom.

6. When ready baked, dust the croissants with the caster sugar and serve.

Baking time: approx. 20 minutes
Electric oven: 200° C
Gas oven: mark 3
Convection oven: 180° C

Per croissant approx. 8 g P, 10 g L, 42 g G = 312 kcal (1 314 kj)

Tasty
Snacks

Hamburger

For 4 servings:
6 white rolls
600 g/1 lb mixed minced meat
Salt
Pepper
3 onions
Oil, for frying
2 cooking tomatoes
4 leaves of green lettuce
4 tbsp mayonnaise

1. Gently heat up 4 of the hamburger rolls in the oven and soak the other 2 in water.
2. Season the minced meat to taste with the salt and pepper.
3. Peel the onions and slice one into rings and chop the other into cubes.
4. Place the onion rings to one side, then mix the onion cubes with the soaked rolls (press out the excess water first) and the minced meat and knead everything together well.
5. Roll the minced meat mass into small balls, press down into flat hamburger shapes and then fry in hot oil on both sides until cooked through.
6. Wash the tomatoes, cut out the hard stalk flesh and chop into thick slices.
7. Slice the 4 hamburger rolls in half and place a lettuce leaf on each of the bottom halves.
8. Place the ready fried hamburgers onto the salad, top off with the tomato slices and onion rings.
9. Finish with a tablespoon helping of mayonnaise, make a sandwich with the other roll half on top and serve.

Preparation time:
approx. 25–30 minutes

Per serving approx. 15 g P, 27 g L, 99 g G = 724 kcal (5 043 kJ)

82

Cheeseburger

For 4 servings:
4 Hamburger rolls
1 white roll
1 onion
450 g/1 lb mixed minced meat
Salt
Pepper
Oil, for frying
2 cooking tomatoes
4 cheese slices
Tomato ketchup

1. Gently bake the hamburger rolls until crisp. Soak the white roll in water. Peel the onions and chop into cubes.
2. Add the minced meat to a bowl and season to taste with the salt and pepper.
3. Press out the excess water from the roll and then add together with the onions to the minced meat and knead everything together.
4. Make 4 flat hamburgers out of the meat mass and then fry in hot oil on both sides.
5. Wash the tomatoes, cut out the hard stalk flesh and chop into thick slices.
6. Slice the hamburger rolls in half. Place the ready fried hamburgers onto the bottom roll half and then top off with the tomato and cheese slices.
7. Place the cheeseburger half onto a baking tray and bake on the middle shelf of a preheated oven until the cheese melts.
8. Finally pour some tomato ketchup onto the cheese and make a sandwich with the top half of the roll and serve.

Preparation time:
approx. 25–30 minutes
Electric oven: 225° C
Gas oven: mark 4
Convection oven: 200° C

Per serving approx. 36 g P, 48 g L, 70 g G = 553 kcal (2 325 kj)

Perogees

For 4 servings:
1 onion
60 g/2 oz mushrooms
Butter, for frying
1 jar of sliced bell peppers
(preserved –125 g/4^1/$_2$ oz)
250 g/9 oz minced meat
Salt
Pepper
250 g/9 oz (1 pkt) ready-made dough
1 egg white
1 egg yolk
Lard, to grease baking tray

1. Peel the onions and chop into small cubes.
2. Trim and wash the mushrooms and cut into cubes.
3. Melt the butter in a frying pan and fry the onions and mushrooms.
4. Remove the onions and mushrooms from the pan and leave to cool.
5. Drain the pepper pieces through a sieve and chop into cubes. Combine the pepper and mushrooms with the minced meat and knead everything together. Season to taste with the salt and pepper.
6. Remove the dough from its packaging and roll out flat.
7. Cut circles (diameter: 10–12 cm/ 4–4^3/$_4$ in) out of the dough.
8. Add the filling to the middle of the circles, and then brush the edges with egg white. Fold the dough circles together into half moons, brush the egg yolk over the dough rolls and place on a greased baking tray.
9. Bake the stuffed rolls in a preheated oven on the middle shelf for 15–20 minutes.

Preparation time:
approx. 30 minutes
Electric oven: 200° C
Gas oven: mark 3
Convection oven: 180° C

Per pirogee approx. 19 g P, 33 g L, 30 g G = 251 kcal (1 055 kj)

Spicy Filled Pasties

For 4 servings:
150 g/5 oz steak fillet
150 g/5 oz cooking potatoes
1 red onion
1 tbsp chopped thyme
Salt
Pepper
250 g/9 oz (1 pkt) ready-made dough
Flour, for preparation
1 egg, separated

1. Wash the steak under running cold water and then dab dry. Chop the meat into cubes.
2. Peel the potatoes and chop into cubes.
3. Peel the onions and also chop into cubes.
4. Mix the thyme together with the meat, potatoes and onions and season to taste with the salt and pepper.
5. Place the dough on a flour-covered work surface and then roll out enough to cut out 4 circles with an 18 cm/7 in diameter.
6. Add the filling to the middle of the circles, and then brush the edges with egg white. Fold over the dough in half and pinch down the ends to make meat pasties.
7. Brush the dough with whisked egg yolk and bake in a preheated oven on the middle shelf until they turn golden brown. Even if the meat still has a slightly pink colour and is slightly rare, it can still be eaten.

Preparation time:
approx. 30 minutes
Electric oven: 170° C
Gas oven: mark 2
Convection oven: 160° C

Per serving approx. 16 g P, 7 g L, 35 g G = 208 kcal (1 209 kj)

Garlic Bread

For 1 loaf:
1 baguette
3 cloves of garlic
125 g/9 oz butter
Salt
Pepper
125 g/4^1/$_2$ oz grated cheese

1. Make diagonal slices into the top of the bread about 2 cm/^{3}/$_4$ in apart.
2. Peel the garlic and chop into small cubes or press.
3. Add the butter to a mixing bowl and whisk until thick and creamy.
4. Fold the garlic into the butter. Season to taste with the salt and pepper.
5. Spread the garlic butter in the cuts in the loaf.
6. Sprinkle the cheese over the bread and then place onto a baking tray and bake on the middle shelf of a preheated oven until the cheese melts.

Preparation time:
approx. 25 minutes
Electric oven: 225° C
Gas oven: mark 4
Convection oven: 200° C

Per 100 g approx. 9 g P, 20 g L, 32 g G = 373 kcal (1 568 kj)

Herb Bread

For 2 loaves:
2 baguettes
1 onion
250 g/9 oz butter
150 g/5 oz (1 pkt) frozen mixed herbs
Salt
Pepper
A pinch of curry powder
Lemon juice

1. Cut the baguette into slices leaving them in one position so that they can be sandwiched together again afterwards.
2. Peel the onions and chop into small cubes.
3. Add the butter to a mixing bowl and whisk until thick and creamy.
4. Add the herbs, onion cubes, spices and a squirt of lemon juice to the butter and mix everything together.

5. Spread the herb butter onto each bread slice and sandwich the pieces together again.
6. Wrap the bread in aluminium foil and bake in a preheated oven for approximately 15 minutes.

Preparation time: 30 minutes
Electric oven: 225° C
Gas oven: mark 4
Convection oven: 200° C

Per 100 g approx. 5 g P, 18 g L, 37 g G = 353 kcal (1 486 kj)

Baguette

For 3 loaves:
Dough:
500 g/1 lb 2 oz wholemeal wheat flour
21 g/$^3/_4$ oz ($^1/_2$ cube) yeast
15 g/$^1/_2$ oz salt
150 g/5 oz fresh clotted cream
200 ml/14 fl oz lukewarm water
Extras:
Flour, for preparation
Approximately $^1/_2$ l/18 fl oz water

1. Sift the flour into a mixing bowl, crumble in the yeast, add the salt, clotted cream and water and knead everything together into a smooth dough.
2. Cover and leave the dough to rise for approximately 45 minutes. Knead the dough well and leave to rise for a further 30 minutes.
3. Cut the dough into 3 equal portions. Roll each portion into a ball on a flour-covered work surface and then stretch into thick lengths.
4. Leave to rise once again, roll back into the desired length, and then place on a baking tray covered with greaseproof paper.
5. Cover and leave the dough to rise for approximately 15 minutes. Make diagonal cuts in the top of each loaf with a sharp knife.
6. Bake the loaves in a preheated oven on the middle shelf for approx. 25 minutes. Place a bowl of hot water on the bottom shelf of the oven.

Preparation time:
approx. 35 minutes
(plus leaving time)
Electric oven: 200° C
Gas oven: mark 3
Convection oven: 180° C

Per 100 g approx. 8 g P, 6 g L, 48 g G = 281 kcal (1 175 kj)

Pepper Baguette

For 4 servings:
1 baguette
150 g/5 oz fresh clotted cream with herbs
$^1/_4$ green bell pepper
$^1/_4$ yellow bell pepper

1. Slice the baguette in half lengthwise and then again width wise. Heat up in a preheated oven for approx. 4 minutes.
2. Remove the 4 slices, spread with a thick helping of clotted cream and then cover with the thinly sliced pepper pieces. Serve warm.

Preparation time:
approx. 15 minutes
Electric oven: 200° C
Gas oven: mark 3
Convection oven: 180° C

Per serving approx. 7 g P, 13 g L, 32 g G = 278 kcal (1 163 kj)

Shrimp Baguette

For 4 servings:
1 baguette
150 g/5 oz fresh clotted cream with garlic
125 g/4$^1/_2$ oz cooked shrimps

1. Slice the baguette in half lengthwise and then again width wise. Heat up in a preheated oven for approximately 4 minutes.
2. Remove the 4 slices and then spread a thick helping of clotted cream on top and cover with the shrimps. Serve warm.

Preparation time:
approx. 10 minutes
Electric oven: 200° C
Gas oven: mark 3
Convection oven: 180° C

Per serving approx. 13 g P, 13 g L, 32 g G = 304 kcal (1 271 kj)

Index